Sì, Parliamo Italiano!

Globalization of the Italian Culture in the United States
and the Increasing Demand for Italian Language Instruction

Vincenzo Milione

&

Christine Gambino

CALANDRA INSTITUTE TRANSACTIONS

CALANDRA INSTITUTE TRANSACTIONS is a series dedicated to studies and analyses that are longer than the usual journal article and shorter than the usual monograph. It will publish manuscripts that fall within these parameters and that deal with any aspect of Italian Americana.

Library of Congress Control Number: 2009933249

CALANDRA INSTITUTE TRANSACTIONS
VOLUME 1

ISBN 0-9703403-3-8
ISBN 978-0-9703403-3-7

©2009 by the Authors and the
John D. Calandra Italian American Institute

published by
John D. Calandra Italian American Institute
Queens College/CUNY
25 West 43rd Street, 17th Floor
New York, NY 10038

TABLE OF CONTENTS

LIST OF GEOGRAPHICAL MAPS IN APPENDIX A

ACKNOWLEDGEMENTS

The authors wish to thank Dr. Anthony Julian Tamburri, Dean, and Dr. Fred L. Gardaphe, Distinguished Professor, of the John D. Calandra Italian American Institute for their comments on previous drafts of this paper.

In addition, we would like to acknowledge the essential contributions of Itala Pelizzoli, Carmine Pizzirusso, and Phyllis Tesoriero of the John D. Calandra Italian American Institute.

PREFACE

This study constitutes a first of a kind, as it examines, first of all, how we might arrive at a more accurate number of people who speak Italian in the United States. In so doing, Christine Gambino and Vincenzo Milione look at the social surveys available to the public and analyze those figures against the background of a century-long evolution of the speaking, studying, and teaching of Italian nationwide. What the reader of this study will ultimately come to understand is that the socio-linguistic landscape for Italian is actually much more broad than we might have thought, precisely because the current tools available to us are, simply stated, out-dated and, to some degree, dismissive willy-nilly of the current situation at hand.

Some of the results demonstrate that (1) the numbers of people reported to speak the language is significantly under-estimated, and (2) scope of who actually speaks the language is, historically speaking, limited in scope, since the social surveys such as the Census have always asked *de facto* qualificatory questions with tags such as what language is spoken "at home" or if it is the "primary" language spoken. As Gambino and Milione demonstrate, such questions can only restrict the numerical results, thus ignoring those instead who, for other reasons still, speak the language on a daily basis either at work or in other situations that do not fall within the boundaries of the strictly familiar or personal.

Proof of the *necessity* of Italian as a *practical*, quotidian language was, to be sure, emphatically underscored by New York City's Mayor Michael R. Bloomberg's Executive Order 120 (22 July 2008). The order requires all city agencies to provide translation assistance to those linguistically dependent on the top six languages spoken other than English by New Yorkers, which include: Spanish, Chinese, Russian, Korean, Italian, and French Creole. In guaranteeing access to programs, services, and activities for our limited-English-proficient sisters and brothers, there is a new Customer Service Group housed in the Mayor's Office of Operations, which works in concert with the Mayors Office of Immigrant Affairs in order to assist in the application of Executive Order 120.

Six month after this encouraging news, the Italian language community received instead a disheartening message with regard to the Advanced Placement Program in Italian. On January 6, 2009, the College Board announced its decision to discontinue the AP Program in Italian after its first three years, along with three other exams ("*Four AP Courses and Exams Discontinued After the 2009 Administration.* 2008-09 will be the final year in which AP French Literature, AP Italian Language and Literature, AP Latin Literature, and AP Computer Science AB courses and exams will be offered."). It did state that if the requisite funds to continue the program were forthcoming, it would consider continuing the AP in Italian.

Gambino and Milione's study also has a function in this regard. It provides greater rationale, for instance, as to why, on a micro level, the AP in Italian should be continued, and, in turn, on a macro level, why Italian needs to be taught on a greater scale nationwide. For example, during the first three years of the Advanced Placement in Italian there was much good news. The percentage of overall growth was indeed impressive: from 2006 to 2007, growth was at 2.8%; the difference from 2007 to 2008, we saw, was an admirable 17.5%.[1] We may surely feel a sense of accomplishment as a community of Italian educators. However, we need to continue the work that we have done during this past year. This work, we can all agree, has been a group effort, which resulted in constructive dialogue among more people and organizations.

What has been especially uplifting with regard to this current and future challenge of ours, has been, for one, the proactive work on the part of the Italian government, from the Embassy in Washington, DC, to the various Consulates and Institutes, among whom I would include: Francesco Maria Talò, Consul General of Italy in New York; Marco Mancini, First Counselor at the Embassy of Italy in Washington; Luigi De Sanctis, Director of the Education Office at the Embassy of Italy in Washington; Alfio Russo, Director of the Education Office at the Consulate General of Italy in New York.[2] These efforts, when combined with those of the teaching community, can only end in positive results for a variety of reasons.

---

[1] The results for the 2009 AP Exam, instead, were not yet available when this study went to press.

[2] Their activities were joined by the more recent contributions of Louis Tallarini, president of the Columbus Citizens Foundation, and those by Margaret Cuomo, president of the then newly formed Italian Language Foundation, of these past six months.

First, the Italian teaching community and the community at large have begun to construct what we can only assume will be a sustained conversation on the issue of the AP as well as other issues. Second, and in a more general sense, this conversation begins to bridge the proverbial town-gown gap. Third, the Italian, Italian/American, and Italophile communities become more knowledgeable of the social position of Italian as a mode of daily communication, a situation that is significantly more extensive, as we read herein, than one might readily believe. Fourth, as these same communities become more familiar with the Italian-language teaching community, the actual profession of teaching Italian gains even greater currency as a professional choice.

These four reasons are some of the basic issues to which we must now continue to strive in this age of "border crossing"; these listed above are, for sure, some of the new borders we need to cross in order to progress successfully with regard to the teaching profession. And the results of Gambino and Milione's study only underscore the need for us as a community to move forward with these and other goals in mind. We must indeed strive to ensure that Italian, especially for the general United States collective consciousness, (1) becomes a language of study on the same level of the so-called canonical languages such as Spanish, French, and German, and (2) is recognized, as we saw in this study, as that functional language *qua* communicative tool it clearly is.

With regard to the teaching of Italian as a choice of profession, a general profile of the Italian high school teacher was recently compiled by three California members of the American Association of Teachers of Italian: Adriana Benvenuto (Granada Hills High School), Teresa Fiore (California State University Long Beach), and Ida L. Nolemi-Lanza (San Pedro High School).[3] It is, for the most part, a descriptive profile that can be readily modified to reflect the numerous geographical areas in which we should encourage students to enter the teaching profession, especially Italian. As we all know, there is a significant need; in the recent past there have been numerous calls for teachers of Italian in the public schools. To some extent, one might say we got caught off guard, and for good reasons. Namely, if we look at the ACTFL report released in 2002 (Jamie B. Draper and June H. Hicks, "Foreign Language Enrollments in Public Secondary Schools"), we see that enrollments in Italian in U.S. public high

---

[3]See http://www.aati-online.org, and click on "High School Programs."

schools for the decade 1990-2000 rose from 40,402 to 64,098, an increase of over 60%. In like fashion, enrollments at the college level saw an incredible increase within the past sixteen years. From 1990 to 2006 enrollments increased from 49,699 to 78,368, a similar increase of over 60%. Our work in the training and formation of teachers, that is to say, is cut out for us!

So, where might we begin? I suggest we first take a step back, pause, and then look within ourselves as Italian language teachers, parents, members of the Italian, Italian/American, and Italophile communities—those of us who, simply, love all things Italian! We need to be sure that as we move forward we do everything we can in order to guarantee that Italian not only survives but, indeed, thrives for decades to come, as enrollments of the past two decades are clear indications of how Italian can grow.[4] It is, that is, now incumbent upon the larger Italian, Italian/American, and Italophile communities (teaching and non) to take one step further, a giant one to be sure. We need to come together, assess what these past few years have wrought in terms of the strategies adopted, hone those that have proved most beneficial, and develop further a new, more inclusive plan that will lead us to our end goals. Such strategies and goals should include, first and foremost:

(1) Raise greater awareness of the teaching of Italian in general and, specifically, the Advanced Placement Program in Italian within the larger Italian, Italian/American, and Italophile communities nationwide. As this study goes to press in mid-year 2009, it is ever so clear that there is an awareness gap within our communities;

(2) Work with our Italian/American legislators at all levels of government—local, statewide, and nationally. This is where our elected officials need to step up to the plate, in a manner similar to what the New York state legislators have done for the past thirty years with regard to Italian/American studies and demographic issues within the City University of New York, in particular, and across the state, in general;

(3) Conduct a fund-raising campaign that—in addition to the grass-roots campaign that was waged for the Advanced Placement Program in Italian—includes direct contact, through expert-informative discussions concerning the world of Italian pedagogy and its various aspects, with the numerous individuals, foundations, and companies that hold a deep interest in Italian culture and language here in the United States and who are also in the financial position to assist in the cause.

---

[4]This obviously includes programs such as the Advanced Placement Program in Italian or any other form a national exam might take.

Especially with regard to numbers 1 and 3 above, The Italian Embassy in Washington, DC and its numerous Consulates, Educational Offices, and Cultural Institutes throughout the United States can serve as sites for such encounters, as they constitute a ready-made national network. Together with AATI representatives, members of the various *Uffici Scolastici*, the various "enti gestori" (e.g., the IACE in New York with whom I collaborate), and those such as NIAF, OSIA, UNICO, ILICA, ILF, the network becomes, to a certain degree, fail-safe.[5]

As we saw above, while enrollments have proven to be most impressive at public school and college levels, the future of the Advanced Placement Exam in Italian is now literally on the chopping block after only three years in existence. It stands as an example of how other matters with regard to the teaching of Italian might turn if we do not give it our utmost attention.[6] The upshot, then, is that by gathering together our respective professional talents and abilities, we all need to develop further strategies, as I mentioned above, that will lead us to our end goals. In order to expedite this process, as we did on a smaller scale, at an April 19, 2008 meeting at the Calandra Institute, representatives of national associations of Italian Studies, of Italian/American Culture and Heritage (e.g.,

---

[5]The complete names are: IACE (Italian American Commission on Education), NIAF (National Italian American Foundation), OSIA (Order Sons of Italy in America), UNICO, ILICA (Italian Language Inter-Cultural Alliance), ILF (Italian Language Foundation).

[6]Now is the time for our greater Italian and Italian/American communities to be candid about the actual status of the Advanced Placement Program in Italian and move forward as an integral force. As I had indicated in the Fall 2008 AATI Newsletter, the loss of this program places at a clear disadvantage those students who have opted for Italian over the so-called canonical languages: those languages that have more currency, we've been told, within the greater United States collective consciousness.

The College Board's recent decision to move forward with their original considerations of last April 2008, to discontinue AP in Italian, reiterates the message that Italian is indeed in a category different than French, German, and Spanish, as implicit as that message may be. While it is true that they have, in the words of their January 8, 2009 letter, "suspended" the AP in Italian for "the 2009-10 academic year," let us not gloss over the fact that their communiqué contains absolutely no guarantee that the Program will be reinstated even if, as they say, "the funding partnerships needed to support an AP Italian program arise." Their communiqué continues, in fact, by stating that the "Board of Trustees will *consider* renewing work to develop and offer the AP Italian course and exam" (emphasis added). We fully understand their use of the verb "consider"; like any commitment of this magnitude, they need to be cautious. We also fully understand that such caution on their part, in turn, only underscores the urgency for us to be sure that what we do offer the best guarantee possible that will lead us to our overall mission of securing an Advanced Placement Program in Italian.

NIAF, OSIA, UNICO, ILICA, ILF), and the Italian Embassy in Washington, DC, should come together and engage in those necessary preliminary talks we need to have before we move forward and develop, *una volta per tutte*, a plan for a national campaign that will achieve the goals described above. To be sure, the ACTFL and MLA reports, together with Gambino and Milione's study, are proof positive that the ground is indeed fertile and ready to be cultivated in this regard.

All of this inevitably speaks to an overall commitment on the part of the Italian and Italian/American lay and professional communities with regard to Italian culture and its many facets. As many of us have stated *ad nauseam*, first and foremost is our language. If we do not know the language, we simply cannot access a greater part of that culture. Furthermore, for those of us who are children and grandchildren of those who spent weeks in steerage, a greater knowledge of Italian affords us greater knowledge to the *hows* and *whys* such immigration took place. Namely, we place ourselves in the advantageous position of being able to take possession of our own history and, in the end, enhance our own self-history.

As both a community at large and a teaching community, we are at a crossroads, to be sure. We have the highest enrollment numbers ever at both the K-12 and college levels. We also are in greater need of support, moral and financial, to ensure that the success of the last twenty years continues. Such support has numerous potential sources; we simply cannot look in one direction only or, for that matter, at one sole funding source. This, to be sure, thus constitutes one of our newer challenges as Italian Americans: cultural philanthropy. To date, we have not fared well in this regard.

The Italian/American community, especially, must now, more than ever, step up to the plate and support grand projects dedicated to the imparting of knowledge of our history and culture; and here I have in mind entities such as centers, institutes, and/or museums. This, of course, brings us to other areas in dire need of cultural philanthropy: namely, the lack of Italian/American names on (a) college and university libraries, (b) colleges of arts and humanities, and (c) named professorships, just to name a few areas. I cannot underscore the *humanities* aspect of this message of mine, precisely because in very few places, indeed, do we find the names of our ethnic brethren associated with funding the arts, the humanities, named professorships, and Centers for Italian and Italian/American studies.[7]

Such philanthropy geared toward the support of Italian language and culture must be a group effort that results in constructive dialogue among more people and organizations, governmental and not, now more than ever before. We need to embark on this new journey in continued and congenial dialogue while eschewing any counterproductive politics of denigration and dismissal. As I said before in a message to the AATI listserve, an overwhelming majority of high school teachers and college professors have all worked assiduously and selflessly over the years in their efforts to maintain an excellence in teaching and research at all levels and in all areas of Italian studies. The fruits of such labors simply must be brought to harvest in the most expeditious of manners.

At the risk of repeating myself, I shall close this preface as I did in a blog in 2008 on the portal *i-Italy.org*. Italian culture extends well beyond the realm of fashion and food! In underscoring the significance of Italian cultural artifacts throughout the centuries, I point to France's Musée du Lourve, one of that country's most grandiose, prized possessions (one that is chock full of art from every corner of the world), which is ubiquitously represented by the icon of an Italian oil painting that measures 30 × 21 inches. *A big job for such a small painting!*

Anthony Julian Tamburri, Dean
JOHN D. CALANDRA ITALIAN AMERICAN INSTITUTE

---

[7]For example, the funding of the Advanced Placement Program in Italian is as valid an investment as the various medical centers and business schools that carry Italian names. Yet, when the opportunity rose, no one individual came forward, as some have with regard to other funding possibilities.

Executive Summary

The Italian language has undergone several changes since the early immigrants first introduced it to the United States. Many Italian immigrants who spoke regional dialects did not pass on their native language because they felt it was a corruption of Italian. Learning Italian at home resulted in additional corrupted "dialects" that made it difficult for immigrant children to speak to each other in Italian (and in some cases resulting in "Brooklynese" which was understood across dialects). In the early 1940s, the Italian immigrant was intimidated in speaking the native language because of public scrutiny in speaking the enemy language during WWII. The post-war Italian descendants benefited from the expansion of the education system in the United States, and many Italian descendants sought learning the Italian language as a career path to teaching and to socio-economic upward mobility, creating a resource for Italian language instruction.

As Italian Americans intermarried, their descendants sought Italian language classes especially if they came from families with multiple ancestries. Post-war Italy underwent another renaissance where it became a major industrial country exporting its products worldwide with much of the glamour of the Italian artistic and technical culture. The multi-cultural interest in the Italian culture has resulted in an increased demand for the Italian language not just by later multi generational Italian Americans but by other global cultures seeking a relationship with Italian culture. This research demonstrates that in spite of the decreased use of the Italian language within Italian American homes over the generations, the interest in the Italian language has increased within American homes. Major findings include:

- The number of people in the United States who can speak Italian is at least three times the often-cited Census estimates of Italian speakers, which only report how many people speak Italian as their primary language at home.
- There are more than three million (3,000,000) people in the United States who speak Italian, which would be comparable to the French and German speakers in the United States if they would have experienced the same level of instruction as the Italian language students. However, the number of Italian speakers in the United States would increase to nearly 6 million (6,000,000) if the same amount of instruction were available to Italian language students as has been available to French and German language students.

- There is a continual decline in number of people speaking Italian as the *primary language at home*. The biggest decline in Italian language is seen in the New York Tri-State Area, where the population of Italian American descendants is also decreasing showing more intra-country movement of Italian Americans to other states, where future generations of Italian Americans will need to rely in classroom instruction for learning the Italian language.
- Suburbanization and intra-country migration underlie many geographic effects on Italian language prevalence. In New York City, Italian Americans are more likely to speak and understand Italian than their counterparts in the suburbs of New York and other rural regions of the nation. However, there is still a large percentage of elderly Italian Americans in urban areas (more than 1 of 6 in New York City) who speak Italian at home and benefit from the younger generation learning Italian in school.
- Italian-American intermarriages have resulted in an increase of Italian-American multiple ancestries with subsequent generations showing increased enrollment in Italian language classes.
- The younger generation (age 5-17) speaking Italian at home is much less than adults (over 18 years of age), underscoring the increasing need for Italian language education in schools. This is becoming more critical since the Italian-American population is increasing nationwide.
- One third (33%) of all adult Italian speakers in the United States are not of Italian ancestry and come from diverse cultures. Italian language classes appear to have as many non-Italians learning Italian. Global interest in Italian culture is increasing in the arts, technology, business, and international relations.
- Of the new Italian immigrants to the United States, 22% originate from Latin American countries. Although their primary home language may be Spanish, many also speak Italian and/or pursue Italian language instruction in schools.

INTRODUCTION

Language is a marker of group and community identity, and a tool for political and social unity. This study examines the prevalence of Italian in the United States, New York City and surrounding Tri-State area[1], which includes the greater New York metropolitan area: i.e., Northern New Jersey, Long Island, Connecticut, and parts of eastern Pennsylvania. Trends over time between the years 2000 and 2006 are examined, as are cross-sectional analyses describing aspects of Italian speakers.

The Italian language has undergone several changes since the early immigrants first introduced it to the United States. The language was predominately imported to this country through the many dialects of the immigrants, rather than the standard Italian now taught in most schools offering the language. Many Italian immigrants who spoke regional dialects did not pass on their native language to their children because it was considered to be a corruption of the standard Italian language. Learning Italian dialects at home made it difficult for immigrant children to speak to each other in Italian (and in some cases resulting in a patois, such as "Brooklynese," in order to cut across the dialects). In the early 1940s, the Italian immigrant was intimidated when using their native language because of public scrutiny in speaking the enemy language during World War II (DiStasi, 2001). The Post World War II Italian descendants, instead, benefited from the expansion of the education system in the United States. Many Italian Americans, having an affinity for the Italian language and interest in the teaching profession, saw Italian language instruction as a logical way to enter academia. As Italian Americans intermarried, their descendants sought Italian language classes especially if they came from families with multiple ancestries. In a study conducted by Milione (1991), in Westchester County, New York, it was found that increases in Italian-American multiple ancestries were positively cor-

---

[1]The Tri-State area is the area defined by the U.S. Census as the New York-Northern New Jersey-Long Island Consolidated Metropolitan Statistical Area (CMSA) which includes parts of New York, New Jersey, Long Island, and Pennsylvania. The CSMA is composed of Primary Metropolitan Statistical Areas (PMSAs) which in turn are made up of counties, parts of counties, and/or towns. See United States Census Bureau (2000), "Metropolitan Areas and their Geographic Components in Alphabetic Sort, 1990 and 2000 Population, and Numeric and Percent Population Change: 1990 to 2000."

related with enrollment in Italian classes.

Post World War II Italy underwent another renaissance as it became a major industrial country exporting its products worldwide, which built upon Italian fashion and technological development. More recently, for many students, learning Italian has been an attempt to reconnect with their roots. The multi-cultural interest in Italian culture has resulted in an increased demand for the Italian language not just by later multi-generational Italian Americans but also by other global cultures seeking a relationship with Italian culture.

SOURCE DATA FOR ITALIAN LANGUAGE ANALYSIS

UNITED STATES CENSUS DATA

The United States census decennial survey is administered every ten years for the entire population, but only a sample of Americans receive a census data questionnaire with detailed demographic questions consisting of a sampling of one out of twenty households, or a 5% sample (U.S. Census Bureau, 2004). All Italian Americans receive a short questionnaire; however, on the short form of the Census, Italian Americans can only identify themselves as "White" and are thus not identified as Italian Americans in the total population counts of the census. On the longer survey questionnaires, there are more specific socio-demographical questions asked, especially about the respondent's ethnic ancestry. Prior to 1980, Italian Americans were identified only as foreign-born or children of foreign-born, presenting an incomplete count of Italian-American descendants in the United States (Gibson and Lennon, 2001). In 1980, ancestry data was reported in the Census Bureau's survey through self-identification that includes multiple ancestries. The respondents who answer Italian as one of their ancestral roots (first or second entry) are counted as within the Italian American population. It is through this ancestry question that Italian Americans are identified not only in government but also in other industries and ranges of life.

The American Community Survey was introduced in 2000 to duplicate the decennial census on an annual basis through a temporal sampling of regional data. Over time, the American Community Survey is intended to produce the same results as the 2010 decennial census data but this will be available annually (U.S. Census Bureau, 2006). The first comprehensive database of the American Community Survey was available in 2006 with sampling refinements to be made up to 2010. About three million households are surveyed each year, from every county in the nation.

When referring to Italian speakers, the decennial U.S. Census and the annual American Community Surveys, at best, record only those who speak Italian as their primary home language. To determine whether a person speaks a language other than English, the Census asks, "Does this person speak a language other than English at home? If so, what is this language?" The U.S. Census and American Community Surveys do not ask about all the languages an individual may be able to speak, read, or understand, but only the *primary* home language. For this reason, when the Census describes 'Italian speakers,' it should *not* be interpreted as including all those many hundreds of thousands of Americans who are able to speak Italian, but do not consider it their primary language spoken at home.

Due to variance in language acquisition in children under five years old, language questions in the U.S. Census are only asked about household members over the age of five. For Census data after the 2000 census, all age groups over five years old have been combined because language data from the annual American Community Surveys using the STF summary files are not split up into age groups at this time, as the 2000 summary data is split into 5-17 year old and over-18 age groups. Additional analysis through individual PUMS (Public Urban Metropolitan System) data can be used for further detail analysis.

General Social Survey

The General Social Survey (GSS) is an annual survey designed to obtain a sample of respondents that represents a larger cross-section of the adult population in the United States, describing detailed social demographic and attitudinal characteristics (Davis and Smith, 2006). Where language questions were not included in GSS prior to 2000, the same language questions are asked of respondents in each year from 2000 to 2006. This enables the GSS language data from these years to be combined for analysis. This results in a combined sample size of 7,327 GSS respondents (including 482 Italian Americans and 50 Italian language speakers) in the weighted sample. In analyzing GSS data for this study, anyone reporting Italian as their first, second, or third ancestry was considered to be of Italian ancestry.

The General Social Survey asks language questions many different ways than the census surveys. Like the U.S. Census, it asks what language a respondent primarily speaks at home, but, in addition, it asks all respondents: "Do you speak any language other than English? If so, which language or languages?" It is possible for the respondent to name up to two different non-English languages providing a conceptual advantage. However, the GSS has other limitations compared to the U.S. Census. The GSS samples a much smaller number of people than the Census, and includes only adults aged 18 years and over. Because of small sample sizes, data from GSS surveys from 2000 through 2006 were combined for this present analysis. In addition, prior to 2006, all GSS respondents were fluent in English, or they would have been excluded from the survey. In 2006, almost all GSS respondents were fluent in English except for a small group that took the survey in Spanish. Therefore, GSS does not include persons from other cultures who may speak Italian but are not fluent in English or Spanish, including populations of Indians, Ethiopians, Nigerians, Russians, etc. who are known to also speak Italian.

Diagram 1 summarizes the data sources used in studying the utilization of the Italian language in the United States.

Diagram 1: Data Analysis

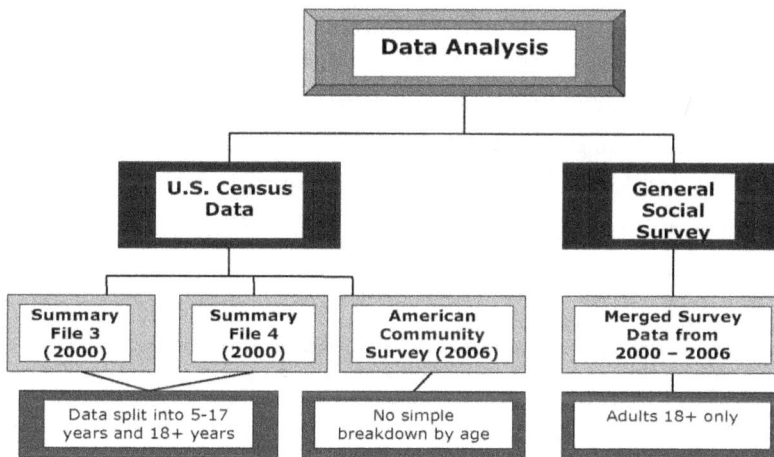

GEOGRAPHICAL ANALYSIS OF ITALIAN ANCESTRY

In order to understand how Italian is being spoken at home, and how this has changed in recent years, this study looks at three geographical areas. First, the study looks at Italian speakers in New York City, where many first-generation Italian immigrants still reside. Second, the Tri-State Area captures the suburbanization of the Italian-American community, and later generations, many of whom have multiple ancestries. Third, the study examines the entire United States, where there is a mixture of the later immigrants and multigenerational descendants of Italians. Using decennial Census data, Figure A exhibits percentages of Italian Americans, by age group, for the United States, Tri-State Area, and New York City, showing the proportion of the population in each region over five years old who report having Italian ancestry. This was determined by dividing the number of persons of Italian ancestry by the total number of people. Italian Americans made up 5.54% of the overall United States population over five years old in 2000, and this proportion was higher in the Tri-State area (15.96%) and within New York City (8.81%).

FIGURE A

Percent of Total Population (Age 5+ Years) with Italian Ancestry, by Age Group

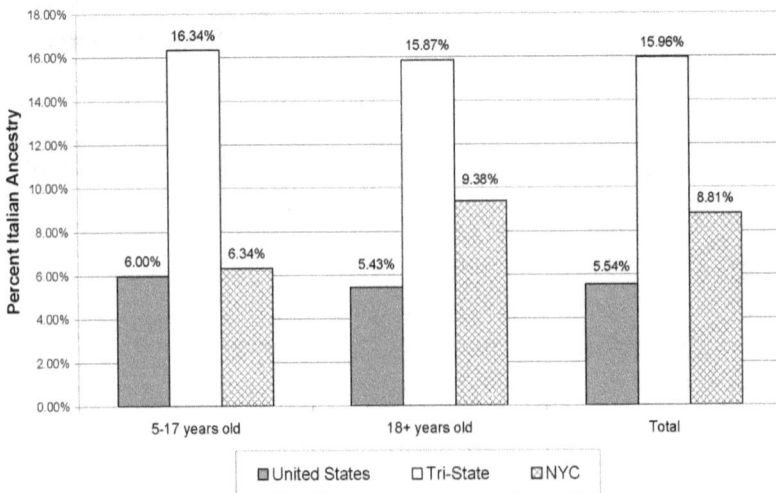

Source: Census 2000 SF 3 and SF 4.

24

Figure B, in turn, shows that between 2000 and 2006, the number of Italian Americans in the United States (over 5 years old) grew 13.56%. This increase in Italian-American population growth may also reflect the increasing ethnic identity growth among the Italian-American community nationwide. This is in direct contrast to what was predicted by Richard Alba (1985), in his much quoted book *Italian Americans: Into the Twilight of Ethnicity*, that Italian-American ethnicity would decline. In six years the number of Italian Americans in the Tri-state area (over 5 years old) fell 15.11%, and the number of Italian Americans in New York City (over 5 years old) declined 3.54%.

Figure B shows these rates of population change for Italian Americans in each geographic area between 2000 and 2006 in terms of the percent change from 2000 numbers. These changes in the New York Tri-State region and New York City may indeed represent an intra-country migration of Italian Americans to the southwest and southeast regions of the U.S., where in fact the Italian-American population has grown. Furthermore, the overall growth in Italian Americans in the U.S. may also be partly attributable to increased awareness of and pride in Italian identity in the U.S., leading to greater reporting of Italian ancestry in the Census survey.

FIGURE B

Percent change in Population Reporting Italian Ancestry (ages 5+ years), from 2000 to 2006

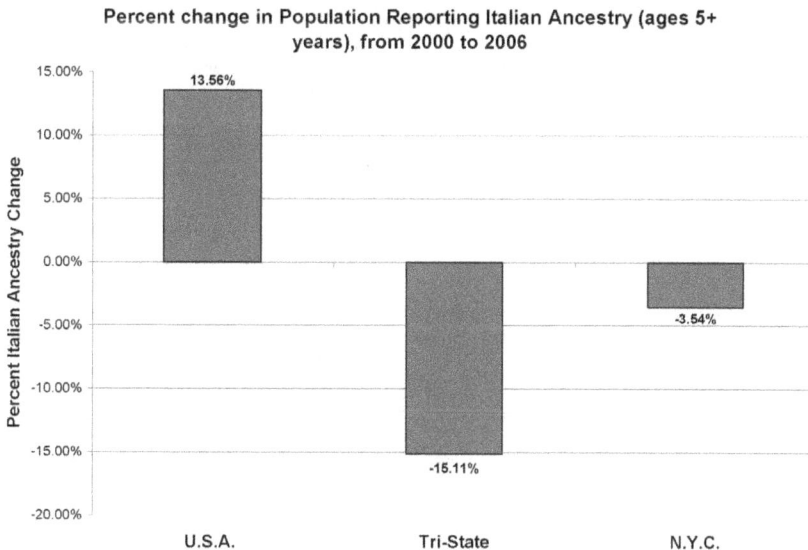

Source: Census 2000 SF 3 and SF 4, 2006 American Community Survey.

25

ITALIAN LANGUAGE SPEAKERS AT HOME

Figure C shows the proportion of Americans who claim Italian ancestry and who also report that Italian is their primary language spoken at home. This percentage was determined by dividing the number of Italian speakers over five years old in each region by the number of people of Italian ancestry over five years old in each region, with the assumption that those who do report speaking Italian as their primary language at home are also of, at least partially, Italian descent. As Figure C shows, the proportion of Italian Americans who do speak Italian at home varies widely by geographic region, with a much higher proportion of New York City Italian Americans speaking Italian at home than in the Tri-State area as well as in the United States overall. This is due in part to the suburbanization of the Italian-American community in recent decades and to the aging Italian-American community in urban areas. Many Italians who immigrated to the United States initially settled in high-density city centers. Their descendants who succeeded economically and/or professionally tended to migrate to the suburban neighborhoods surrounding these cities, providing fewer opportunities to maintain the use of the Italian language. In fact, between 1970 and 1980, 40% of the Italian Americans in New York City moved to the suburbs surrounding New York City (Milione, 1995).

FIGURE C

Percent of Population (Age 5+ Years) With Italian Ancestry Who Speak
Italian at Home, by Age Group

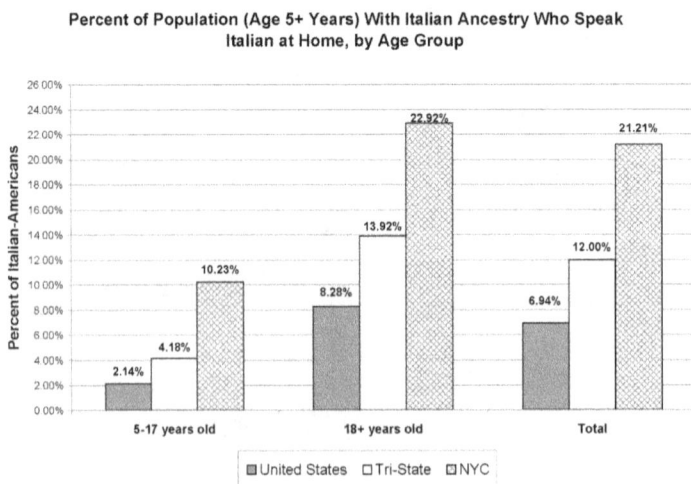

Source: Census 2000 SF 3 and SF 4.

26

Figure D shows the change in the percentage of people over age five speaking Italian as the primary language at home between 2000 and 2006. This change in number of Italian speakers between 2000 and 2006 is represented in terms of percent change from 2000 numbers. The number of people speaking Italian at home decreased between 2000 and 2006 in all geographic regions examined, both in terms of absolute number of Italian speakers and percentage of people of Italian ancestry who spoke Italian at home. In those years, the number of Italian speakers declined 17.84% in the United States overall, 28.81% in the Tri-State area and 21.39% in New York City. This pattern suggests that so far in this decade, the number and proportion of families of Italian ancestry who speak Italian at home are decreasing, and thus there is a corresponding increase in families of Italian ancestry who instead speak English at home.

It is important to remember that this overall decline in the "number of Italian speakers" is only referring to people who speak Italian as their *primary* language at home. No such decline has been documented among Americans who learned Italian in school, or who know the language but speak English or another language more frequently. On the contrary, converging evidence shows an increase in the study of the Italian language in schools (Draper & Hicks, 2002; Furman, Goldberg & Lusin, 2006).

FIGURE D

Percent Change in Number of People who Primarily Speak Italian at
Home (Age 5+ Years) from 2000 to 2006

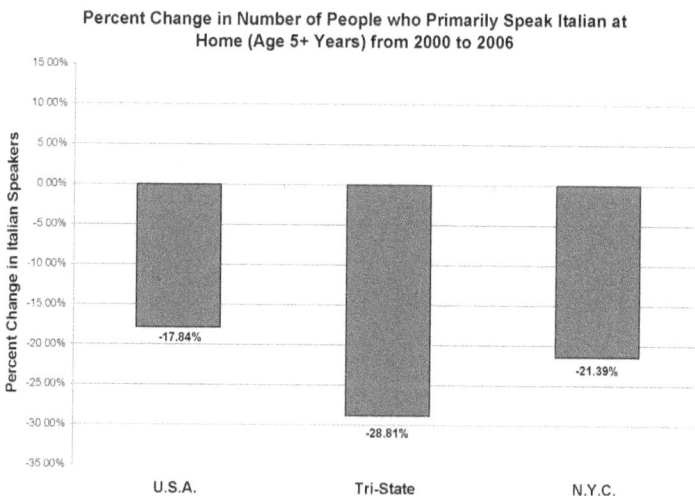

Source: Census 2000 SF 3 and SF 4, 2006 American Community Survey.

Understandably, most people speaking Italian at home are of Italian ancestry. Therefore, much of the decline in the prevalence of Italian home speakers must be due to lower numbers of Americans of Italian ancestry speaking Italian at home. Suburbanization and the need to speak English for work and school certainly play a part. First-generation immigrants from Italy to the United States are increasingly fewer, and new immigrants of Italian ancestry may have traveled a complicated route to get here. More recently, many first-generation Italian Americans have not come here directly from Italy, but instead, for example, may have lived in Latin American countries or other global regions, consequently becoming familiar with a variety of languages and not beholden to speaking Italian at home. For example, 22% of recent immigrants of Italian ancestry came to the United States from Latin America (Milione, 2006).

To understand how Italian has evolved from the early immigrant settlements to suburbanization and dispersion throughout the country, it is important to look at differences in trends regarding the number of Italian Americans who are speaking Italian at home in the United States, Tri-State, and New York City. Figure E examines change between 2000 and 2006 in the percentage of Italian Americans who are also speaking Italian at home in each geographic region, the assumption being that people who speak Italian as the primary home language are all, or almost all, of Italian ancestry. This percentage was calculated by dividing the number of Italian speakers over age five in each region by the number of persons over age five reporting Italian ancestry. In each geographic region, the proportion of Italian Americans who also spoke Italian at home declined in these six years. This again reflects that the aging Italian immigrant population, who primarily speak Italian at home, is disappearing.

FIGURE E

Percent of Italian Americans (Age 5+) Who Primarily Speak Italian at Home, From 2000 to 2006

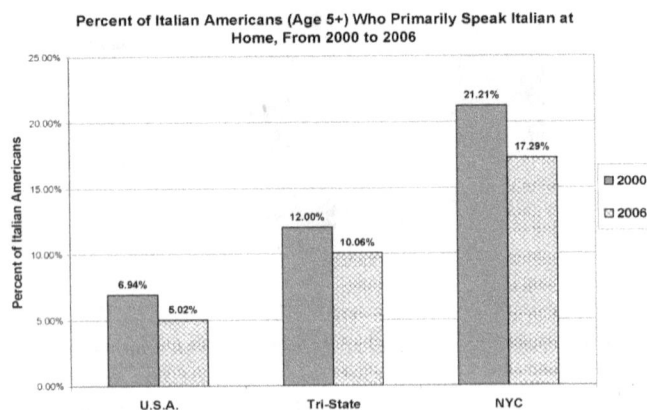

Source: Census 2000 SF 3 and SF 4, 2006 American Community Survey.

Italian Language Usage in the United States

Table 1 in Appendix B shows that in the United States in 2000, the total population over 5 years old was 262,375,152 (53,096,003 aged 5-17 years, and 209,279,149 aged 18 and over). Of these, 14,538,472 reported that they are of Italian ancestry, including 3,184,637 aged 5-17 years, and 11,353,835 aged 18 and over.

In 2000, 5.54% of the total United States population over age five was of Italian ancestry. Looking just at school-age children between 5 and 17 years old, 6.00% of school-age children in the U.S. were of Italian ancestry. For those in the U.S. aged 18 years and older, 5.43% were of Italian ancestry. This higher percentage among Italian-American youth underscores that Italian heritage and ethnicity are not disappearing, and may indeed increase with greater awareness of Italian identity. In particular, in the 1980s and 1990s, there was an increased proliferation of Italian-American organizations and their local chapters, such as the National Organization of Italian American Women (NOIAW), National Italian American Foundation (NIAF), Order of the Sons of Italy in America (OSIA), UNICO, and others which reached out to the community, and worked toward counteracting negative stereotypes presented in the media (Commission for Social Justice, 1991). Such outreach efforts generated more media attention and public interest in Italian-American affairs. Identification with Italian ethnicity may surely be different than it was in the past, but it has not disappeared.

In the U.S. in 2000, there were 1,008,370 people over age five who spoke Italian as their primary language at home. The probability of speaking Italian at home was higher for those Italian-American adults aged 18 and over than for school-aged Italian Americans. In fact, 68,029 of those speaking Italian at home were aged 5-17 (or 2.14% of the Italian-American population in the U.S. aged 5-17 years), while 940,341 were 18 years or older (or 8.28% of the Italian-American population in the U.S. aged 18 and over). Nationwide, there is a larger decrease in speaking Italian from generation to generation compared to the Tri-State area and New York City. In the greater United States, the significantly lower percentage of youth speaking Italian at home compared to the older generation highlights more of a need for nationwide programs in Italian language instruction, since there are fewer opportunities among later-generation Italian Americans to learn it at home.

In the United States (Table 2) the population over age five identifying themselves as being of Italian ancestry grew 13.56%, from 14,538,472 to 16,509,824 people between the years 2000 and 2006. The number of Italian home speakers declined 17.84% from 1,008,370 to 828,524, even as the population of Italian Americans in the U.S. increased considerably. The proportion of Italian Americans in the U.S. who spoke Italian at home declined from 6.94% in 2000, to 5.02% in 2006.

ITALIAN LANGUAGE USAGE IN THE NEW YORK TRI-STATE AREA

As shown in Table 3, in the year 2000, the total population over 5 years old in the New York Tri-State area was 19,775,438 (3,802,455 aged 5-17 years, and 15,972,983 aged 18 and over). In this Tri-State population, 3,155,394 reported having Italian ancestry, including 621,272 aged 5-17 years, and 2,534,122 aged 18 and over.

In 2000, almost one out of six people in the Tri-State area had Italian ancestry. Looking just at school-age children between 5 and 17 years old, 16.34% of school-age children in the Tri-State area were of Italian ancestry. For those in the Tri-State area aged 18 years and older, 15.87% were of Italian ancestry. This higher percentage of Italian-American youth, compared to the adults, may show either a higher fertility rate among Italian Americans in the Tri-State area, which is unlikely, or an increase in families identifying their children as Italian American in the Tri-State area.

In the New York Tri-State Area in 2000, the proportion of Italian Americans who spoke Italian at home was higher than for the United States overall, but the picture is similar in terms of Italian being more commonly spoken at home by adults age 18 and over. In the Tri-State area there were 378,623 people over age five who spoke Italian at home. Of these Italian speakers, 25,952 were aged 5-17 (or 4.18% of the Italian-American population in the Tri-State area aged 5-17 years), while 352,671 were 18 years or older (or 13.92% of the Italian-American population in the Tri-State area age 18 and over). This is a large difference between age groups, suggesting that in the Tri-State Area, adult Italian Americans are generally not passing down the language to school-age children at home, suggesting a greater need for more instruction in school-based Italian language studies. More research is needed to understand why these families are not passing the language down to their children.

Between 2000 and 2006, the Tri-State area experienced a decline in the Italian-American population as well as the overall population, with numbers of Italian Americans over five years old declining 15.11% from 3,155,394 to 2,678,576. Changes for the Tri-State area between 2000 and 2006 are reported in Table 4 in the Appendix.

In the Tri-State area, the number of Italian speakers over age five declined 28.81% in six years, from 378,623 to 269,525. However, the proportion of Italian Americans over age five in the Tri-State area who primarily spoke Italian at home declined by a much smaller percentage, from 12.0% in 2000 to 10.06% in 2006, again showing that the outward migration from the New York Tri-State area predominately consists of later generations of Italian Americans who do not speak Italian. The difference shows that the remaining aging Italian immigrants are also being left behind in the Tri-State area as their descendents migrate to other regions of the country.

ITALIAN LANGUAGE USAGE IN NEW YORK CITY

Table 5 reports numbers and percentages of persons of Italian ancestry and Italian speakers in the five boroughs of New York City. In New York City in 2000, the total population over 5 years old was 7,475,602 people (1,397,597 aged 5-17 years, and 6,078,005 aged 18 and over). Of these New York City residents over age five, 658,579 reported that they are of Italian ancestry, including 88,642 aged 5-17 years, and 569,937 aged 18 and over.

In 2000, 8.81% of the total New York City population over 5 years old was of Italian ancestry. Looking just at school-age children between 5 and 17 years old, 6.34% in NYC were of Italian ancestry. For those in NYC who were 18 years and older, 9.38% were of Italian ancestry. This difference between age groups, with a lower prevalence of Italian-American youth, shows the aging of Italian Americans in New York City. Obviously, since many later-generation Italian-American descendents moved to the suburbs, many of the Italian Americans remaining within New York City are aging post-war immigrants. As a result, in New York City in 2000, the proportion of Italian Americans who spoke Italian at home was higher than either the United States overall or the suburban Tri-State area. The proportion of Italian Americans who spoke Italian at home was also greater for those aged 18 and over than for those aged 5-17 years. In NYC, there were 139,698 people over age five who spoke Italian at home, representing 21.21% of those reporting Italian ancestry. Of these Italian speakers, 9,072 were aged 5-17 (or 10.23% of Italian Americans in New York City aged 5-17 years), while 130,626 were 18 years or older (or 22.92% of Italian Americans in New York City aged 18 and over). These numbers show that a more traditional, connected Italian-speaking community still exists within the five boroughs. Over one out of five Italian Americans in New York City still use Italian as their primary language in the home, and this is not counting thousands more who speak Italian in other contexts. However, the Italian Americans who speak Italian at home in NYC are more likely to represent an aging immigrant and first-generation population than their descendants.

As shown in Table 6, New York City's overall population over age five increased slightly between the years 2000 and 2006; however, the number of Italian Americans over age five in NYC decreased slightly, down 3.54 percentage points from 658,579 to 635,290 Italian Americans.

In the five boroughs of New York City, the number of Italian speakers over age five declined 21.39% in six years, from 139,698 to 109,817. The proportion of people in New York City of Italian ancestry who spoke Italian at home, while still high compared to the rest of the nation, declined from 21.21% in 2000, to 17.29% in 2006.

ITALIAN LANGUAGE SPEAKERS IN THE UNITED STATES
A BROADER PICTURE

Looking at Italian language speakers at home does not present an accurate picture of the prevalence and magnitude of Italian speakers in the United States. As stated earlier, the U.S. Census data is limited in that it describes only those who speak Italian as their *primary* language at home. The General Social Survey (GSS), instead, asks language questions in many different ways. Like the U.S. Census, it asks what language a respondent speaks at home; however, it also asks all respondents: "Do you speak any language other than English? If so, which language or languages?" This provides the opportunity to identify and then study Italian-language speakers from any racial or ethnic ancestry.

Diagram 2 shows how Italian is used in the United States. As discussed above, older immigrants use the language to communicate at home, whereas newer immigrants from Italy and other countries brought with them both the Italian language and a notable interest in passing on the Italian language to others. Simultaneously, over the years, American communities have developed interest in learning and using Italian in cultural and business environments. Currently, Italian speakers include all of these groups, many of whom may or may not speak Italian at home; that is, they may use Italian in various situations that range from domestic to international settings.

Diagram 2:
Italian Language in the United States

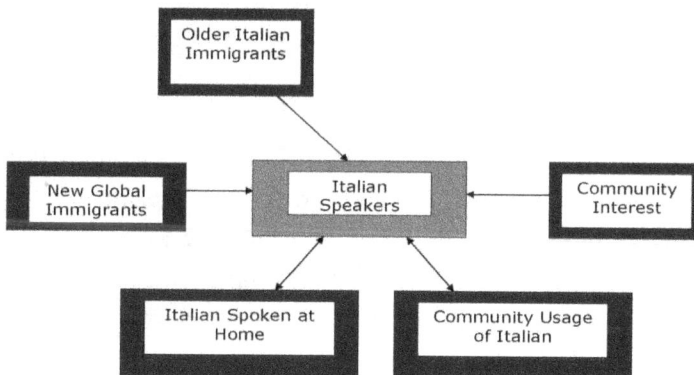

35

In fact, by including all the racial and ethnic ancestries from the General Social Survey within the United States global society, the results show that only about one out of three American speakers of Italian actually reports speaking Italian as his or her primary language at home. Table 7 and Figure F show that of all Italian language speakers in the U.S., one-third reported speaking Italian as their primary language at home. This percentage was different for speakers of Italian language versus other non-English language speakers in the United States. Figure F shows that 41.3% of non-Italian speakers of a language other than English spoke the language at home. This may be due to the new immigrants to the United States who may be more likely to speak Asian languages and Spanish in the home.

FIGURE F

All Adult Italian Speakers in the U.S.A.

All Adults Able to Speak a Foreign Language in the U.S.A. (excluding Italian speakers)

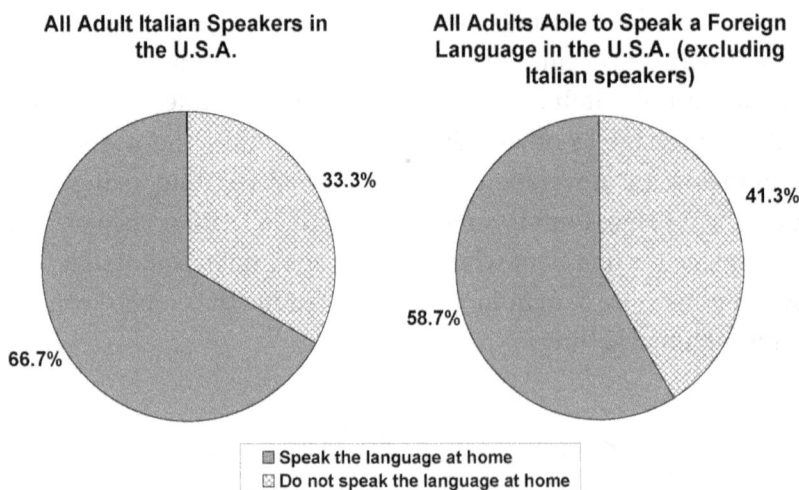

33.3%

66.7%

41.3%

58.7%

☐ Speak the language at home
☒ Do not speak the language at home

Source: General Social Survey 2000-2006.

Compared to other "foreign" language speakers, Italian speakers are less likely (33%) to speak Italian as the primary language at home. In effect, only one-third of Italian speakers in the U.S. speak Italian at home. However, as stated earlier, the U.S. Census only asks about languages spoken as the respondent's primary home language. By including only home speakers, Census reports grossly underestimate the number of people who speak Italian in all contexts.

Since only one-third of all Italian speakers speak Italian as their primary home language, it can be extrapolated that the actual number of all Italian speakers in the United States is probably at least three times greater than the Census estimates that are usually presented. For example, if present 2006 Census estimates there are 828,524 Italian speakers in the U.S., 269,525 in the Tri-State CMSA, and 109,817 in the five boroughs of NYC, then it is likely that in 2006 there are probably close to 2.8 million over the age of 18 years old in the United States who could speak Italian, including over 800,000 Italian speakers in the Tri-State area, with about 330,000 of those in New York City. In Figure G, Census figures are compared to the projected total number of Italian speakers (not just those who primarily speak Italian at home). For this analysis, 2000 Census and 2006 American Community Survey numbers were averaged to produce "Census counts," in order to ensure a valid comparison with the GSS data, for which 2000 and 2006 data were combined.

FIGURE G

Projected Number of Italian Speakers (Age 5+) by
Geographical Region

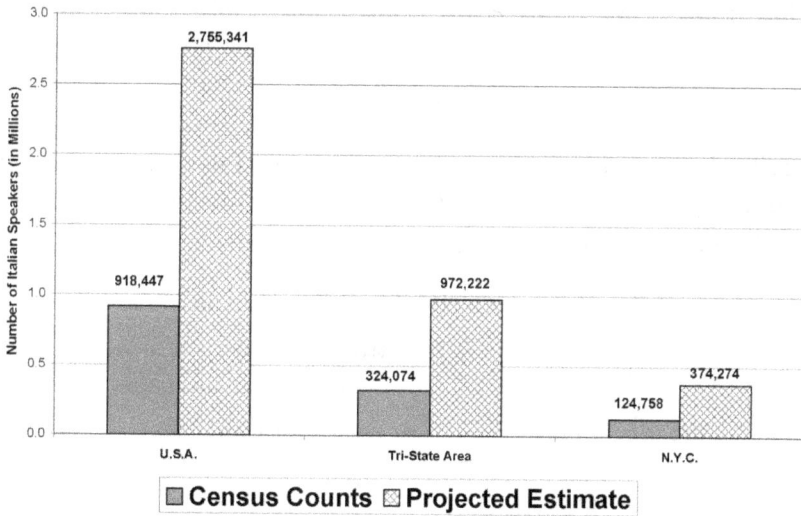

Source: 2000 U.S. Census, 2006 American Community Survey,
and General Social Survey 2000-2006.

The projected numbers show a much more realistic and sizeable group of Italian speakers in the USA. However, this is still an underestimate since younger Italian speakers in the U.S. are probably even *more* likely to have learned Italian at school instead of at home. Therefore, Cen-

37

sus estimates of Italian speakers (based on home-speakers) aged 5-17 should be an even greater underestimate of the real total amount of school-aged Italian speakers than Census estimates of adult Italian speakers. Since 25.6% of all Americans speak another language besides English, and 5.1% of those foreign language speakers use Italian, it is possible that the actual estimate of Italian-language speakers is as high as 2,947,346 people. Further research with school-aged populations is necessary to find out how many more Americans under 18 years are speaking Italian compared to the Census estimate of how many speak Italian as the primary home language. However, the American Council on the Teaching of Foreign Languages (Draper and Hicks, 2002) shows an increase in middle-school and high-school enrollments through the 1990s, indicating that there may be more Americans under 18 years old speaking Italian.

An interesting pattern emerges among Italian speakers in the U.S. as compared to speakers of non-English languages who cannot speak Italian. Of those in the U.S.A. who can speak Italian, two out of three primarily speak English (or another language) at home. As shown in Table 7 and Figure F, Italian speakers are *less* likely than other 'foreign' language speakers to speak Italian at home with their families. However, Italian speakers are *more* likely than other 'foreign' language speakers in the U.S. to have *learned* Italian at home, rather than at school or elsewhere, showing the past history of the lack of Italian language classes in schools. Table 8 and Figure H examine speakers of Italian and speakers of other non-English languages, demonstrating where the languages were learned: in the childhood home, at school, or somewhere else.

FIGURE H

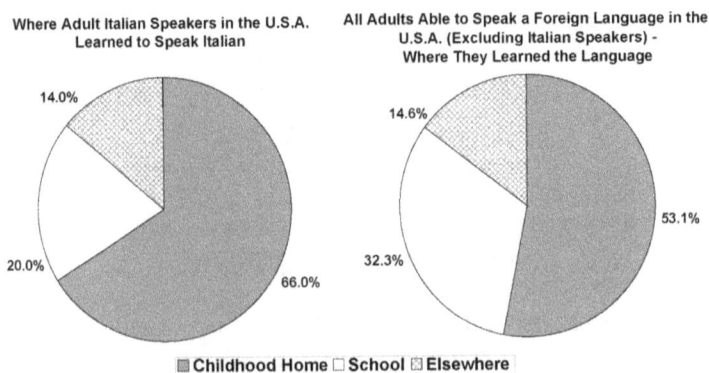

Where Adult Italian Speakers in the U.S.A. Learned to Speak Italian

14.0% 20.0% 66.0%

All Adults Able to Speak a Foreign Language in the U.S.A. (Excluding Italian Speakers) - Where They Learned the Language

14.6% 32.3% 53.1%

■ Childhood Home □ School ▨ Elsewhere

Source: General Social Survey 2000-2006.

Although Italian speakers are significantly more likely than other "foreign" language speakers in the United States to have learned the language at home from parents, grandparents, or other family members, they are less likely to continue this trend by speaking Italian at home and thereby teaching it to their children. This finding may be one of many factors that explain the 17.84% drop in the number of Italian home speakers in the U.S.A. between 2000 and 2006. This indicates that Italian Americans learning Italian at home has decreased but that the descendants are now learning the language outside the home (Draper and Hicks, 2002; Furman, Goldberg and Lusin, 2007).

Of course, one does not have to *be* Italian to speak Italian. The importance of Italian to non-Italians in the U.S.A. is a good example of the globalization of Italian culture in the world. Most adults in the U.S. who speak Italian (72.3%) are of partial Italian ancestry. Table 9 shows various countries of family origin for people in the United States who reported being able to speak Italian, while Figure I shows that nearly one out of three people in the U.S. who speak Italian are not of Italian ancestry. As shown in Table 9, after Italy, the most common countries of family origin for Italian speakers are Germany (8.5% of Italian speakers), Puerto Rico (6.4% of Italian speakers), and Ireland (4.3% of Italian speakers). In this analysis, anyone reporting Italian as his or her first, second, or third ancestry was considered to be of Italian ancestry. A corollary to this mix ancestry is that many of the other cultures combined with the ancestries of Italian Americans may be reflected in their speaking the languages associated with those other heritages.

FIGURE I

Country of Family Origin for Speakers of the
Italian Language in the U.S.A., 2000-2006

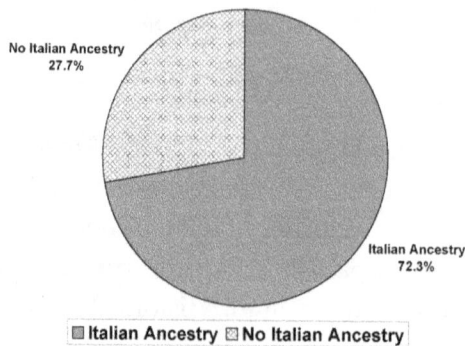

No Italian Ancestry
27.7%

Italian Ancestry
72.3%

☐ Italian Ancestry ☒ No Italian Ancestry

Source: General Social Survey 2000-2006.

39

LANGUAGES SPOKEN BY ITALIAN AMERICANS

As Table 10 and Figure J show, approximately one out of four (26.7%) Italian Americans over 18 years old can speak another language in addition to English, similar to 25.6% of the overall national sample of adults. Many Italian Americans are multilingual: over one out of twelve (8.5%) Italian Americans can speak two or more languages in addition to English. Italian Americans have many reasons to be bilingual or multilingual, indicating an interest both in retaining their cultural heritage, in exploring global cultures, as well as succeeding in fields such as international business and international relations. In recent decades, Italian Americans have benefited from increased education (Milione, DeRosa and Pelizzoli, 2007) and have increased in the diversity of professions, which may facilitate or necessitate multiple language learning.

FIGURE J

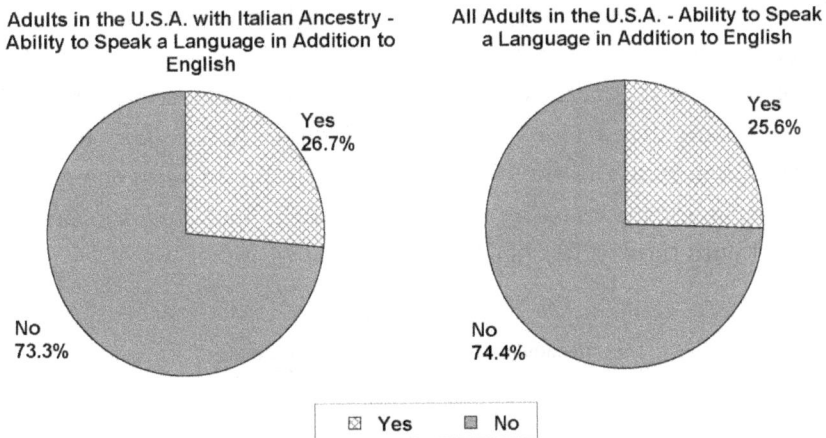

Adults in the U.S.A. with Italian Ancestry - Ability to Speak a Language in Addition to English

Yes 26.7%
No 73.3%

All Adults in the U.S.A. - Ability to Speak a Language in Addition to English

Yes 25.6%
No 74.4%

Yes · No

Source: General Social Survey 2000-2006.

Italian is not the only language an Italian American might learn. Of Italian Americans who speak a language other than English, less than half are able to speak Italian. Excluding Italian, of non-English languages that Italian Americans speak, Spanish is the most common, followed predominately by French and then German. Historically, since Italian was not offered in middle and high schools, Italian Americans had no choice but to select French, Spanish, or German to fulfill language requirements.

Many of the newer immigrants of Italian ancestry are coming from Latin America, contributing to the prevalence of Spanish fluency among Italian Americans. Figure K shows the foreign languages Italian Americans are able to speak, again, not the primary language they speak at home. It is also interesting that Italian Americans are speaking Dutch and Arabic, possibly again showing an interest among Italian Americans in global developments in Africa and the Middle East, where those two languages are more common. Italian Americans are also showing interest in American Sign Language, possibly reflecting the growing popularity of teaching and social work as careers among Italian Americans. People who do not speak English were not included in the General Social Survey. Therefore, recent immigrants who may be of Italian ancestry or who may speak Italian, but have little knowledge of English, are not represented.

FIGURE K

Languages Spoken by Italian Americans (Age 18+) in the U.S.A.

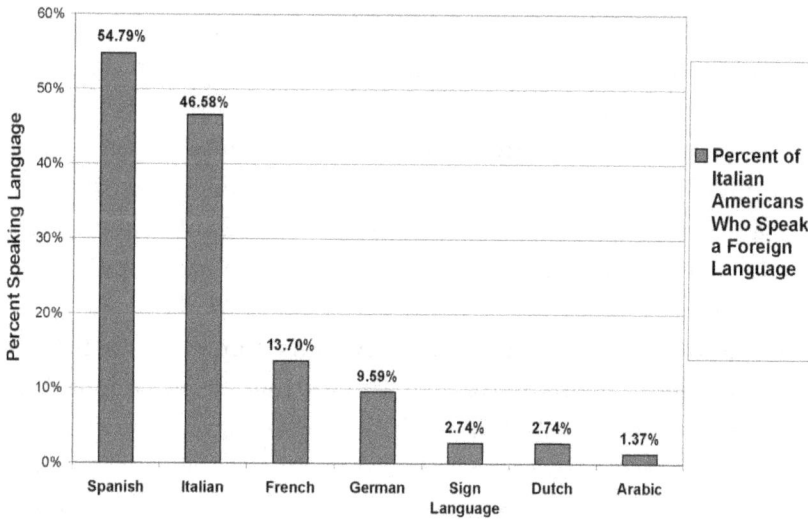

Note: Percentages add up to over 100% because many respondents speak multiple languages.
Source: General Social Survey 2000-2006

The Impact of School Instruction
for Italian Language Speakers

To understand better the growing demand for Italian in the United States and the increasing need for Italian language instruction, we may look to the historical development of French and German language speakers. Historically, French and German languages were usually available throughout the United States for the middle-, secondary-, and university-students' fulfillment of the foreign language requirements in his or her education curricula. Spanish and Asian languages became more available during the 1970s and represent a different and more recent cultural immigration concern for educational institutions. As presented earlier, 46.58% Italian Americans may have opted for Spanish, probably because of its perceived closer relationship to Italian and since most schools did not offer Italian courses. However, many schools would encourage Italian Americans and other Americans to learn French and German by justifying the numerous literary and scientific publications in the disciplines (especially prior to the advent of the Internet, when translations of publications into English were limited.) Apparently there was less regard for, if not ignorance of, the great Italian developments in science and technology, philosophy, and literature, which included the works of Dante and Cesare Beccaria, or the scientific research of Galileo and Enrico Fermi, for instance, compared to the perceived value of the publications of the French Jean-Paul Sartre or the German Neil Bohr.

Using another methodological analysis as compared to the analysis presented earlier to estimate the demand for Italian speakers in the United States, the recent distribution for Italian, French, and German speakers in the United States can also be estimated using the 2006 census data and other results of the 2000-2006 General Social Survey. As discussed earlier, approximately 25.6% of all Americans over 18 years old speak a foreign language. Since the General Social Survey is limited to the 18 years and older population, this analysis will focus on that group who also most likely experienced language instruction in their education studies. Out of the 225,746,458 Americans 18 years or older in 2006, there are 57,791,093 Americans who speak a least one foreign language. Figure L shows that, of all the Americans who speak a foreign language in the United States, 13.7 % speak French, 8.6 % speak German and 5.1 % speak Italian.

FIGURE L

**Percent Within the Population (18+ years) in U.S. who Speak a
Foreign Language and the Language Shown**

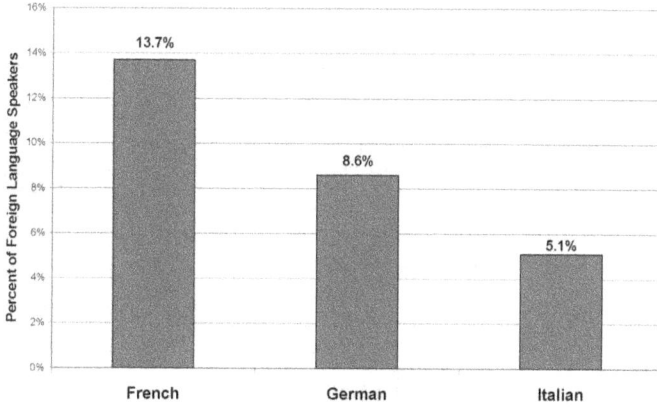

Source: General Social Survey 2000-2006

As shown in Figure M, this incidence of foreign language speakers over 18 years old results in approximately 7,917,380 million French speakers, 4,970,034 million German speakers, and 2,947,346 million Italian speakers. The numbers, on the surface, suggest a larger market interest for French and German than for Italian, therefore minimizing the real interest for the Italian language. However, this difference in the respective language speakers has most likely come about because, historically, school instruction for French and German has been more available than for Italian, as has been demonstrated in reports of language enrollments (Draper and Hicks, 2002; Furman, Goldberg and Lusin, 2007).

FIGURE M

**Projected Total Number in U.S. (Age 18+) Who Speak
the Languages Shown**

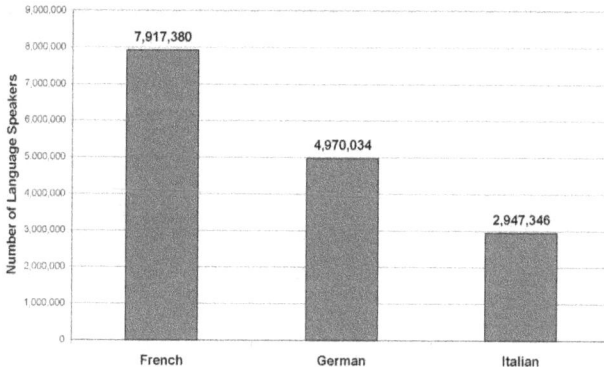

Source: General Social Survey 2000-2006, 2006 American Community Survey

The availability of language instruction in schools is demonstrated by Figure N where approximately 61.2% of the French speakers and 50.5% of the German speakers learned the language in school while only 20% of the Italian speakers learned the language in school. This by itself shows historically how limited the Italian language instruction has been for foreign language students in the United States compared to French and German. Since French and German language instruction has been more available in the United States, then more Americans have had the opportunity to take these languages for their foreign language requirement. German language instruction may have had slightly less interest and utilization than French within the school curriculum because, like Italian and Japanese, it was considered an enemy language during World War II since the U.S. was at war with Italy, Germany and Japan.

FIGURE N

**Percent of Foreign Language Speakers in the U.S. (age 18+)
Who Learned the Language at School**

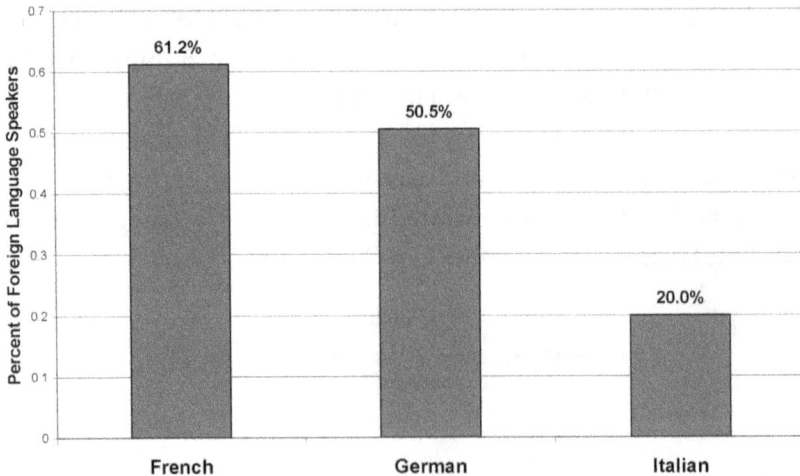

Source: General Social Survey 2000-2006

Actually, if the level of French and German language instruction had been as limited in schools as it was for Italian, the number of French and German speakers would be much less today. Figure O projects the difference of less French and German language instruction if only 20% of the French and German speakers would have learned the language in school. With limited school language instruction, the number of French speakers

44

would only be 3,686,332 million and the number of German speakers would only be 2,952,200 million, which is more comparable to the 2,947,346 million Italian speakers in the United States today. The approximately three million Italian speakers is still an undercount since the 5 to 17 year olds who are now learning Italian in schools are not being counted, for they constitute a growing number of the new Italian speakers.

FIGURE O

Projected Number of Language Speakers (age 18+) in U.S. if All Languages Received the Same Amount of School Instruction as Italian

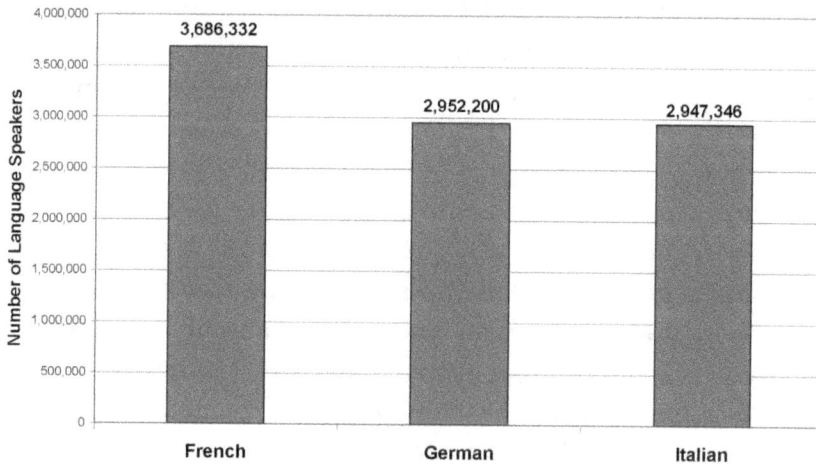

Source: General Social Survey 2000-2006, 2006 American Community Survey

Conversely, if 60% of all the Italian speakers in the United States would have had the opportunity to study Italian in schools today, then the number of Italian speakers in the United States could now be as high as 5.9 million. There is no question that if more Italian language instruction were available in schools, the distribution of Italian speakers would be much higher, providing more opportunities for Americans to participate in the globalization of Italian culture.

SUMMARY AND CONCLUSION

This report uses data from the U.S. Census and the General Social Survey on the prevalence of the Italian language in the United States, Tri-State area, and New York City from the years 2000 to 2006. While it appears that knowledge and use of Italian have been declining in Italian-American homes in the U.S., it nevertheless remains an important mode of communication. Italian language use at home is higher for adults aged 18 years and over than for school-age children aged 5-17 years. This is due, in part, to an aging population of immigrants from Italy, increased multiple ancestry among their descendents, and reduced transmission of the language through use in the family home. Two out of three Italian speakers in the U.S. learned the language from their families, in their childhood home.

Not surprisingly, Italian language use as the primary language at home is highest in New York City, and higher in the New York Tri-State area than in the broader United States, suggesting that in New York City there is a more traditional Italian-American community which maintains the culture developed through its ancestral roots. The importance of Italian is notable among adults in the New York City area, where approximately 23% of people of Italian ancestry speak Italian as their primary language at home. Among the younger generation, about one out of ten Italian Americans in NYC between the ages of 5 and 17 years old speaks Italian at home.

In the Tri-State Area, the impact of suburban migration by Italian Americans on Italian language usage changes is more apparent. In 2000, about one out of six people in the Tri-State Area was of Italian ancestry. Despite these large numbers, use of Italian in the home is decreasing, with about 13% of adult Italian Americans and only 4% of school-aged (5-17) Italian Americans speaking Italian at home in the Tri-State area. Many of the Italian Americans who moved to the suburbs are the later descendents of the earlier Italian immigrants and, for reasons stated earlier, did not learn Italian at home. More suburbanized Italian American communities have led to the increase of multiple ancestries and acculturation into the predominately English-speaking society, thus these numbers should not be surprising. Children of later generations are creating a higher interest in Italian language instruction in school. As early as 1990, it was found that secondary and middle schools in neighborhoods that had higher Italian-American multiple ancestries had the highest enrollment in Italian language classes (Milione, 1991). Since the number of Italian-American youth with mixed ancestry is increasing, there will be a growing demand for Italian language instruction in the new millennium. Additional research is needed to ascertain if this pattern is continuing.

For the approximately 78% of Italian Americans (80% of Italian American school-aged youth) who live outside the NYC Tri-State area, the decline of Italian as a primary home language is even more notable, especially among children aged 5-17. Overall in the United States, about one out of twelve Italian-American adults over 18 still primarily speaks Italian at home, but only about one out of fifty Italian-American school-aged children does.

It is understandable that the use of Italian as the primary language at home declined after many generations since the initial immigration of the 1880s. However, the overall interest and use of Italian has not declined, and instead has seen an increase due to greater interest in learning the language among Americans of many different backgrounds. Approximately one out of three of all the Italian speakers in the United States are non-Italian. Consistently, one out of three of the Italian speakers in the United States learn the language in school or other contexts outside the home. The globalization of the Italian language is further demonstrated among many new non-Italian immigrants to the United States who have prior Italian-language experience. Formal surveys of professors of Italian have not been conducted to document the potential increase of non-Italian American students enrolled within their classes. Only one out of three Italian speakers speaks the language at home, indicating that the number of Italian speakers can be three times more than reported in the census data and can be higher than three million Americans who know Italian.

In fact, a limiting factor in increasing the number of Americans speaking Italian has been the availability of Italian language instruction within the schools. Where approximately 60% and 50% of French and German speakers, respectively, learned the language in school, only 20% of Italian speakers learned the language in school. As stated above, if the level of French and German language instruction had been as limited in schools as it was for Italian, the number of French and German speakers would be much less today: French speakers would only be 3,686,332 million, and German speakers would only be 2,952,200. This is more comparable to the 2,947,346 Italian speakers in the United States today. On the other hand, if 60% of all the Italian speakers in the United States would have had the opportunity to study Italian in schools in the past, the number of Italian speakers in the United States would now be as high as 5.9 million.

The increasingly large percentage of Italian language students of non-Italian or mixed ancestry will affect the demand for Italian language instruction among the multi-generational Italian Americans as well as among non-Italians. In fact, this is a continuation of earlier results showing that in Westchester County, enrollment in high-school Italian classes increased as the number of multi-generational Italian American high school students increased (Milione, 1991).

This is further demonstrated by the growing number of Italian language students taking the Advanced Placement exam within the three years after its implementation. The study of Italian has become more popular in American high schools and colleges, and the number of students taking the exam has grown each year. However, there still have not been enough schools offering the advanced placement (AP) course in Italian or encouraging students to take the exam.[2]

As noted earlier, there is an increase in enrollment in Italian language instruction in schools (Draper and Hicks, 2002; Furman, Goldberg and Lusin, 2007). This is occurring despite, or most likely in part because of, a decrease in use of Italian as a primary home language. The use of Italian has changed over time since the early immigrants introduced it to the United States over 100 years ago. In its current incarnation, Italian is not being spoken in a context of linguistic isolation of an immigrant group, which is how the Census originally studied Italian language speakers. Instead, Italian Americans are now predominately fluent in English, and approximately 12.5% speak Italian with varying degrees of fluency. Today, those who do wish to learn Italian will find that their best option is to learn standard Italian in school.

Many, about one out of three, Americans who speak Italian, are not of Italian origin. If the current composition of Italian classes is a good indicator, then future speakers of Italian in the Americas will be from ever more

---

[2]As this study goes to press, the Advanced Placement Program in Italian has suspended for 2009-2010, possibly reinstated for the 2010-2011 academic year if enough funds become available. There had been an attempt to raise the requested nine-plus million dollars by the Italian Language Foundation, founded in fact to address this issue, but its efforts, unfortunately, did not meet with success in order to avoid the 2009-2010 suspension.

diverse backgrounds. Another likely consequence of the shift from learning Italian at home to learning Italian at school is a possible diminution of the variety of dialects that would be learned at home, in favor of more standard Italian. Instead of having dialects from many regions represented, more Italian speakers in the United States in the future may speak a more standard version of the language. School-based instruction in standard Italian will become ever more critical, as a vital foundation for multi-generational Italian Americans to have a basis for learning more about and appreciating their own personal linguistic heritage. With increased Italian language instruction, more communication in standard Italian will be possible. As a result, more specialized scholars will be needed to document the many dialects of Italian such as Sicilian, Sardinian, Abruzzese, etc. Italian language and Italian American Studies departments should support the instruction of Italian language dialects, including their history.

These findings highlight the increasing importance of school-based and community-based programs for learning Italian, especially for the younger generation. Presently, two out of three adult Italian speakers in the U.S. learned the language from their families, in their childhood home. Transmission of the language at home, from generation to generation, is declining. With this disappearance of everyday use of Italian at home, and Italian Americans continuing to move from traditional inner city communities to suburbs and outlying areas, this may reduce the prevalence of the Italian language in the United States. More schools will need to offer and expand Italian language classes.

In terms of the crisis of the Advanced Placement Program in Italian, this analysis may lend credence for maintaining the program. The U.S. Census shows that in 2000 there were 68,029 children in the United States aged 5-17 who spoke Italian as their primary language at home. However, there were three times more who can speak at least some Italian, a projected total of 204,087, including 136,058 who would not be counted as Italian speakers by the Census because they are not speaking Italian as their primary language at home. Any student proficient in Italian may sit for the AP exam without having to participate in an Italian course, but few students are aware of this opportunity.

As Figure P ultimately demonstrates, there has been an increasing trend in Italian language enrollment at the high-school and college levels between 1958 and 2006. This increase has been more dramatic in recent decades. Between 1994 and 2000 there was a 38% increase in Italian enrollment in American high schools, despite a small decrease in French and German enrollment (Draper & Hicks, 2002). In 2006, there were strong regional differences in Italian enrollment in middle schools and high schools across the U.S. In 2006, 60.8% of Italian language students in public middle schools (grades 7-8) were located in New York State, while 42.1% of Italian language students in public high schools (grades 9-12) were located in New York State (Draper & Hicks, 2002). This concentration of Italian students in New York State public schools may reflect a higher percentage of Italian Americans in New York State, and the greater relative availability of Italian instruction in public schools.

FIGURE P

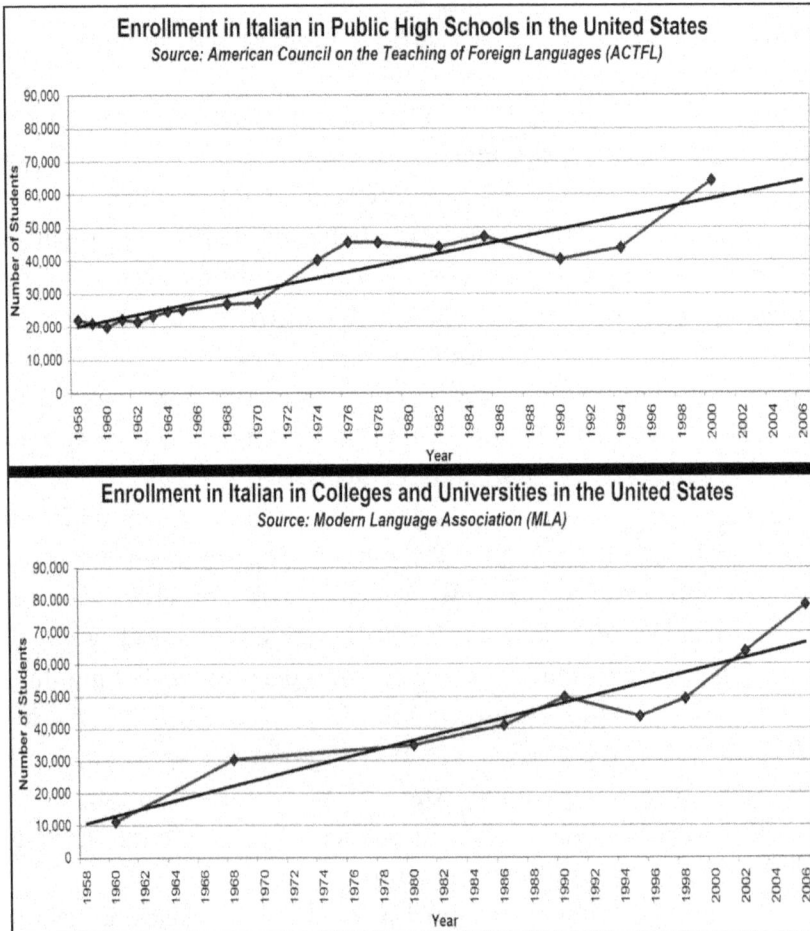

Enrollment in Italian in Public High Schools in the United States
Source: American Council on the Teaching of Foreign Languages (ACTFL)

Enrollment in Italian in Colleges and Universities in the United States
Source: Modern Language Association (MLA)

The number of students taking Italian in colleges or universities in the United States has been increasing, especially during the 1990s. According to the Modern Language Association's report (Furman, Goldberg & Lusin, 2007), 43,760 postsecondary students were studying Italian in 1995, 49,287 were studying Italian in 1998 (an increase of 12.6% from 1995), 63,899 in 2002 (an increase of 29.6% from 1998), and 78,368 in 2006 (an increase of 22.6% from 2002). Many more college and university students may also be taking Italian but are not officially enrolled.

Regional differences in Italian enrollment reflect the relative availability of Italian instruction. Of the 78,368 students taking Italian at the college level in 2006, 41.2% were located in the Northeast. Approximately 18% of these college students enrolled in Italian in 2006 (13,908 students) were located in New York state alone. In New York state, 102 colleges and universities offered Italian in 2006 (Furman, Goldberg & Lusin, 2006).

At the university level, many more students take introductory-level Italian courses than take advanced-level courses. The ratio of introductory students to advanced students is 9:1 (Furman, Goldberg & Lusin, 2006), meaning there are 9 post-secondary students taking introductory Italian for every student taking advanced Italian. Across the top 15 languages studied at the postsecondary level, the ratio of introductory students to advanced students is 5:1, showing a larger difference between introductory and advanced study in Italian than other modern languages (Furman, Goldberg & Lusin, 2006).

With the number of Americans speaking Italian at home declining, and the number of Americans learning Italian at school rising, those who are interested in documenting the significance of the Italian language in the U.S. should be increasingly mindful of how the number of Italian speakers is measured. Organizations which use U.S. Census figures to quantify Italian speakers are likely to give numbers that are gross underestimates of the true number of people who can speak Italian and who are interested in the Italian language.

Even with the best measures, numbers can only give us a taste of the importance of the Italian language in the United States, within the Tri-State area, and throughout New York City. Some significant recent trends are shown, and this should encourage and inform further research on Italian language in order to gather a fuller picture of Italian speakers in the United States, Tri-State area, and New York City.

Historically, part of the problem in measuring language prevalence in the United States is that in the past, Census analysts have viewed linguistic diversity in the United States as somewhat of a negative facet of society, a measure of the linguistic isolation of immigrant groups and their neighborhoods. This attitude has changed somewhat, but improvements have been slow. In 1970, language questions began to be asked of everyone, but prior to 1970 language questions were only asked of foreign-born Census respondents. Over the past century, language questions and concepts in the Census have not changed much, although "primary home language" has replaced "mother tongue" (Gibson & Lennon, 2001). Better data collection and research are needed in order to fully understand how language is a tool for the globalization of society.

REFERENCES

Alba, Richard D. (1985). *Italian Americans: Into the Twilight of Ethnicity.* Englewood Cliffs, NJ: Prentice Hall.

Commission for Social Justice (Order Sons of Italy in America) and John D. Calandra Italian American Institute (1991). *Effective Media Monitoring: How to Deal Effectively with the TV Media.* Bellmore, NY: Commission for Social Justice. Unpublished.

Davis, J. A. & Smith, T. W. (2006). *General Social Surveys, 1972-2006.* Chicago, IL: National Opinion Research Center; Storrs, CT: University of Connecticut.

DiStasi, L. (2001). "How World War II Iced Italian American Culture." In L. DiStasi (Ed.), *Una Storia Segreta: The Secret History of Italian American Internment in World War II.* Berkeley, CA: Heyday Books.

Draper, J.B. & Hicks, J.H. (2002). *Foreign Language Enrollments in Public Secondary Schools, Fall 2000.* Alexandria, VA: American Council on the Teaching of Foreign Languages.

Furman, N., Goldberg, D. & Lusin, N. (2007). *Enrollments in Languages Other Than English in United States Institutions of Higher Education, Fall 2006.* New York, NY: Modern Language Association of America.

Gibson, C.J. & Lennon, E. (2001). *Historical CensusSstatistics on the Foreign-Born Population of the United States: 1950-1990.* Washington, DC: U.S. Bureau of the Census.

Milione, V. (1991). *Westchester County Italian Language Studies: Course Offerings and Student Enrollment by Italian American Population.* New York, NY: John D. Calandra Italian American Institute. Unpublished.

_____. (1995). The Changing Demographics of Italian Americans in New York State, New York City and Long Island: 1980 and 1990. *The Italian American Review* 4.1: 14-36.

_____. (1996). "The Changing Demographics and Geographic Distribution of Italian Americans on Long Island." In K.P. Lavalle (Ed.), *Italian Americans on Long Island: Presence and Impact.* Stony Brook, NY: FI LIbrary.

_____. (2006, September). *Global Education for the Social Economic Development of South America.* Paper presented at the *Consejo Iberoamericano en Honor a la Calidad Educativa,* Buenos Aires, Argentina, September 27, 2006. Unpublished.

Milione, V., De Rosa, C., & Pelizzoli, I. (2007). *Italian American Youth and Educational Achievement Levels: How are we Doing? Revised.* Unpublished report. http://qcpages.qc.cuny.edu/calandra/research/pdf/ 2000hsdropout.pdf.

U.S. Census Bureau (2004). *Accuracy and Coverage: Evaluation of Census 2000 Design and Methodology.* Washington, DC: U.S. Department of Commerce Evaluation and Statistics Administration.

U.S. Census Bureau (2006). *Design and Methodology: American Community Survey.* Washington, DC: U.S. Government Printing Office.

Geographical Distribution of Italian Americans: New York City, New York Tri State Region and United States

The historical immigration of Italian Americans to the United States is well documented. Many of the turn-of-the-century Italian immigrants migrated through the major seaports of New York City, Baltimore and New Orleans. These cities were opportunities for Italian immigrants to find employment and adapt to the new culture.

With subsequent generations, the Italian American population in these cities grew highly visible and their descendants moved to the regional suburbs and subsequently throughout the country. The later Italian immigration wave after World War II to the United States was not as large, but appreciable enough to add to the Italian Americans in these geographical areas. Understandably, many of the second wave immigrants settled near the established Italian-American communities due to family ties and cultural and language affinity.

The later Italian-American descendants, after generations of educational achievements and professional mobility, were able to break family ties to pursue employment opportunities and an improved quality of life. They adapted to geographical regions in the United States where the Italian Americans were not as numerous and not dependent on Italian language. In some cases, the elderly Italian Americans followed their children and kept some of the immigrant culture active including speaking Italian. The following describes the geographical distribution of Italian Americans today within New York City, the New York Tri-State region, and the United States, to see where Italian Americans are likely to be speaking Italian.

Italian American Geographical Distribution in New York City

The largest immigration of Italians was to New York City. Many of the Italians that arrived to New York City through Ellis Island found their way to the nearby downtown Manhattan into the tenements of Little Italy neighborhoods. Eventually, with the advent of streetcars and the subway, they migrated out to East Harlem and Brooklyn. From these neighborhoods, the Italian immigrants migrated to the Bronx, Queens, and, with the opening of the Verrazano Bridge, to Staten Island. By the 1970s, Italian Americans were dispersed throughout New York City with approximately 25% of the New York City population of Italian ancestry.

From 1970 to the 1980s, approximately 40% of the New York City Italian-American population migrated out to the suburbs of Long Island, Westchester, Connecticut and North New Jersey. In recent years Italian Americans represent only 8.2 percent of the population of New York City, with many Italian Americans in concentrated neighborhoods within the five boroughs of New York City, and with fewer Italian Americans remaining in Manhattan and the Bronx.

Figures 1 through 5 demonstrate where Italian Americans are presently residing in Manhattan, Bronx, Brooklyn, Queens and Staten Island, respectively. The geographical maps show where the Italian American population is at equal or less than the average city percentage representation (less than 8.6%), equal or more than the average city percentage representation, up to approximately double the representation (8.6% to 20%) and where the Italian American communities are highly dense, with approximately 3 or more times the average city percentage representation.

In Manhattan there are 1,537,195 residents with 84,956 Italian Americans representing 5.5% of the population. Most of the Italian Americans are located on the southwestern part of Manhattan in the neighborhoods of West Village, Soho, Tribeca and Battery Park City, and the Eastside communities of Gramercy, Murray Hill, and Lenox Hill. However, small pockets of high-density neighborhoods with 10% to 20% of the residents still are visible in Clinton, Upper West Side and Yorkville. These high-density communities are bordered by Italian-American neighborhoods where the percentage representation of Italian Americans is approximately twice the city average. The low-density (less than city average of approximately 9%) Italian-American neighborhoods are in the East Village, Little Italy, Chinatown, East Midtown, Clinton, and the Upper West Side to Morningside Heights.

In the Bronx, there are 1,332,650 residents with 69,289 Italian Americans representing 5.2% of the population. Most of the Italian Americans are located on the eastern part of the Bronx in the neighborhoods of Throgs Neck, Schuylerville, Edgewater Park, City Island, and Westchester Square with approximately 30% or more of these residents being of

Italian ancestry. However, small pockets of high-density neighborhoods are still visible in Clinton, Upper West Side and Yorkville. There are some remnants of Italian-American neighborhoods in Belmont and North Riverdale where there are areas of Italian American residency, with the percentage representation approximately twice the city average of 10% to 20% of the population. There is a scattering of low-density (less than city average) Italian-American neighborhoods in the Belmont, Co-Op City, Woodlawn, and Kingsbridge communities.

On the average, Brooklyn has 2,465,326 residents with 183,868 Italian Americans representing 7.5% of the population. Large concentrations of Italian Americans (30% or more of the residents) are located on the southern part of Brooklyn in the neighborhoods of Bay Ridge, Bensonhurst, Bath Beach, Gravesend, Marine Park, Mill Basin, and parts of Sheepshead Bay. However, small pockets of high-density neighborhoods are still visible in East Williamsburg and Carroll Gardens. These high-density communities are bordered by Italian-American neighborhoods where Italian Americans are highly represented, with the percentage representation of Italian Americans at approximately twice the city average (10% to 20% of the residents) in Bay Ridge, East Bensonhurst, and Sheepshead Bay, as well as Park Slope and Brooklyn Heights. There are scatterings of low-density Italian-American neighborhoods (less than city average of approximately 9%) in Sunset Park West, Greenpoint, Starrett City and Brighton Beach.

In Queens, there are 2,229,379 residents with 187,540 Italian Americans representing 8.4% of the population. Large concentrations of the Italian Americans (30% or more of the residents) are located on the southwestern part of Queens in the neighborhoods of Middle Village, Glendale, Ozone Park, Lindenwood, Howard Beach and the northwestern communities of Whitestone and Murray Hill. However, small pockets of high-density neighborhoods are still visible in Floral Park and Steinway. These high density communities are bordered by Italian-American neighborhoods where there are highly represented areas of Italian Americans with the percentage representation twice the city average (10% to 20% of the residents) in the communities of Ridgewood, Woodhaven, Bellerose, Bayside, Douglaston, Little Neck, College Point, Maspeth, Sunnyside, Astoria, Rego Park, Queensboro Hill and Breezy Point. There is a scattering of low-density Italian-American neighborhoods (less than city average of 9%) in Flushing, Jackson Heights, Sunnyside, Astoria, Corona, Forest Hills, Ridgewood, Fresh Meadows, and Douglaston.

In Staten Island, there are 443,728 residents with 167,086 Italian Americans representing 37.7% of the population. Staten Island is typical of how the Italian-American population in New York City was in the 1970s with large concentrations of Italian Americans (30% or more of the residents) located throughout Staten Island in most of the neighborhoods. However, these high-density communities are bordered by a few Italian-American neighborhoods where the percentage representation is approximately twice the city average (10% to 20%) in the communities of Clifton, Fox Hills, New Brighton, St George, Port Richmond, and Arlington. The only communities in Staten Island that have a low-density Italian-American percentage representation (less than city average of approximately 9%) are the Grymest Hill, Clifton, and Fox Hills neighborhoods.

ITALIAN AMERICAN GEOGRAPHICAL DISTRIBUTION IN THE TRI-STATE AREA

Figure 6 and Table 11 clearly show the suburbanization of Italian Americans in the New York, New Jersey, Connecticut and Pennsylvania metropolitan region. In the metropolitan area there are 21,199,865 residents with approximately 3,394,366 Italian Americans representing 16% (one out of six) of the population in the region. The geographical map clearly demonstrates that the New York City counties outside of Staten Island have the least visible percentage representation of Italian Americans. The counties surrounding New York City have more than double or tripled the New York City's percentage representation of Italian Americans, compared to the NYC Boroughs except for Staten Island.

The counties that have nearly double the Italian-American percentage representation of New York City (10% to 20%) include Essex County, Union County, Mercer County, Middlesex County, Passaic County, Rockland County, Fairfield County, Warren County, Somerset County, Orange County and Pike County. The regional counties that have nearly or more than the three times the Italian-American percentage representation of New York City include Bergen County, Sussex County, Morris County, Monmouth County, Nassau County, New Haven County, Ocean County, Suffolk County, and Putnam County. Only Hudson County and Essex County have percentage representation closer to New York City even though the percentage of Italian Americans in these counties is still higher than in New York City.

Interestingly, Staten Island in New York City has the highest representation of all the counties. After Staten Island, the counties with the highest percentage of Italian of Americans in descending order are Putnam County, Suffolk County, Ocean County, New Haven County, Nassau County, and Monmouth County. However, these counties have numerically less Italian Americans than the counties in New York City. The more numerous Italian Americans (greater than 150,000 residents) are in Suffolk County (408,572), Nassau County (319,602), New Haven County (201,069), Bergen County (194,614), Westchester County, (192,226), Queens County (187,540), Kings County (183,868), Richmond County (167,086) and Fairfield County (159,785).

ITALIAN AMERICAN GEOGRAPHICAL DISTRIBUTION IN THE UNITED STATES

Figure 7 and Table 12 show the percentage representation of Italian Americans in the United States, by state. In the United States, there are 285,230,516 residents with approximately 15,730,277 Italian Americans representing 5.5% of the population. The geographical map clearly shows that the highest percentage of Italian Americans is in the North East region. States with the highest percentage of Italian Americans, in descending order, are Rhode Island (19.0%), Connecticut (18.6%), New Jersey (17.9%), New York (14.4%), Massachusetts (13.5%), Pennsylvania (11.6%), Delaware (9.3%), and New Hampshire (8.5%). There are also higher-than-average percentages of Italian-Americans in Nevada (6.6%), Vermont (6.4%), Florida (6.3%), Illinois (6.0%) and Ohio (6.0%).

California has 1,450,854 Italian-American residents, but only 4.3% of the population is of Italian ancestry. Despite this relatively low percentage, it ranks among the top five most numerous states with one million or more Italian Americans residing within the state along with New York (2,737,115), New Jersey (1,503,637), Pennsylvania (1,418,465), and Florida (1,003,967). Fifty percent (50%) of the States still have less than 3 percent of the state population who are of Italian-American ancestry. This suggests that residents in those states would need to encounter at least 33 people before meeting one Italian descendant.

GEOGRAPHICAL DISTRIBUTION OF ITALIAN AMERICAN SENIOR CITIZENS

As discussed in the main text of this report, older Italian Americans are more likely to speak Italian at home. Figures 8 to 14 show the neighborhoods where the Italian Americans that are 65 years or older are located in the five boroughs of New York City, the Tri-State region, and the United States. The dark-shaded communities have at least 20% to 50% of the Italian-American population that are 65 years or older. The other communities that have a younger distribution of Italian Americans are shown in mesh shading for 10% to 20% Italian-American senior citizens, or dotted shading for 0.01% to 10% Italian-American senior citizens.

These who were senior citizens in 2000 are likely to have migrated to the United Stated in or before the 1940s, or were born in the United States as children of Italian immigrants who arrived a generation before, as early as the 1910s to 1920s. In either case, there is a high likelihood that these senior citizens speak Italian or had spoken Italian at some point in their history. In many cases, they would identify themselves as Italian speakers at home. In addition, they are more likely to remain in the neighborhoods where they raised their families, while the next generation of children is more likely to move to communities in the surrounding suburban areas or beyond.

ITALIAN AMERICAN SENIOR CITIZENS IN NEW YORK CITY

Figure 8 shows where Italian Americans who are over 65 years of age predominately reside in Manhattan. The highest incidence of Italian-American senior citizens are in the downtown Manhattan neighborhoods of West Village, Chinatown and Battery Park City and the Eastside communities of Gramercy, Murray Hill, with some left in Little Italy where the Italian immigrants originally settled upon arriving to the United States. The younger Italian-American communities are distributed on the East Side and West Side of Manhattan.

Figure 9 shows that the larger concentrations of Italian-American senior citizens in the Bronx are in Throgs Neck, Pelham Bay, Edgewater Park, and Westchester Square. These communities are bordered by Italian-American communities that have 10% to 20% Italian-American senior citizens. There are very few Italian-American communities in the Bronx that have less than 10% senior citizens. There are also isolated communities where there are high concentrations of senior citizens in Belmont, Woodlawn, Wakefield and Kingsbridge.

Figure 10 shows that the larger concentrations of Italian-American senior citizens in Brooklyn are in Bay Ridge, Bensonhurst, Bath Beach, Gravesend, Marine Park, Mill Basin, and parts of Sheepshead Bay. These communities are bordered by Italian-American communities that have

10% to 20% Italian-American senior citizens. There are very few Italian-American communities in Brooklyn that have less than 10% senior citizens. There are also isolated communities where there are high concentrations of senior citizens in East Williamsburg, Carroll Gardens, Windsor Terrace and Starrett City.

Figure 11 shows that the larger concentrations of Italian-American senior citizens in Queens are in Middle Village, Glendale, Ozone Park, Lindenwood, Howard Beach and the northwestern communities of College Point, Whitestone, Murray Hill, Floral Park, Glen Oaks, Bayside, Douglaston, Maspeth, Sunnyside, Astoria, Rego Park, and Queensboro Hill. These communities are bordered by Italian-American communities that have 10% to 20% Italian-American senior citizens. There are very few Italian-American communities in Queens that have fewer than 10% senior citizens. There are also isolated communities where there are high concentrations of senior citizens in Astoria, Steinway, Ridgewood, Woodhaven, and Bellerose,

Figure 12 shows that the larger concentrations of Italian-American senior citizens in Staten Island are in Todt Hill, Emerson Hill, Heartland Village, Old Town, Dongan Hills, South Beach, Port Richmond, Arlington and Grasmere. These communities are bordered by many more Italian-American communities that have 10% to 20% senior citizens. However, in Staten Island there are many more communities that have a younger distribution of Italian American population with less than 10% Italian American senior citizens. There are only two isolated communities where there are high concentrations of senior citizens, in New Brighton and Silver Lake.

ITALIAN AMERICAN SENIOR CITIZENS IN THE TRI-STATE REGION

Figures 13, 14, and 15 show the distribution by county of Italian-American senior citizens within the Tri-State regional states: New York, New Jersey and Connecticut, respectively. The solid shaded counties have the largest percentage concentration of Italian-American Senior citizens. It is obvious that the oldest Italian-American communities (greater than 20% senior citizens) are in New York City. Bordering counties such as Hudson and Ocean County in New Jersey, and Westchester County in New York, also have a high percentage of Italian-American senior citizens with 15% to 20% of the Italian-American community that is over 65 years old.

Many of the further distant counties from New York City have a younger Italian-American population distribution with only 5% to 15% of the Italian American population who are senior citizens, including Nassau, Suffolk, and Putnam counties. The most distant counties in upstate New York, southern New Jersey and eastern Connecticut tend to have very few Italian-American senior citizens with less than 10% of the Italian-American community being 65 years old or older.

ITALIAN AMERICAN SENIOR CITIZENS IN THE UNITED STATES

Figure 16 shows the distribution of Italian-American senior citizens in the United States by statewide population. The older Italian-American populations are in the Northeast states of New York, New Jersey, Connecticut, Pennsylvania, Connecticut, Massachusetts and West Virginia with 10% to 17% of the Italian-American population that are 65 years or older. Interestingly, West Virginia is included due to the early migration of Italian immigrants to the state for mining employment.

In Southern United States, Louisiana also has an older Italian-American population distribution since New Orleans was an early immigrant port of entry to the United States. Florida also has an older Italian-American population, since in more recent years many Italian Americans have retired in the state after employment.

On the West Coast, California and Nevada have an Italian-American community which is more than 10% senior citizens who are 65 years or older. Many of the Italian Americans from the Northeast, Midwest and Southern states migrated to California in the 1960s and 1970s due to open land, Mediterranean climate, job growth, and growth of cities. Similar to Florida, Nevada has become a retirement destination for many Italian Americans.

The remaining 40 states (or 80% of the states) in the country have a younger Italian-American population with less than 10% of the State's Italian community who are 65 years old or older. Although the Italian-American population has gradually grown in many states, many of these latter generation Italian Americans migrated to these states due to employment relocations and multicultural families.

FIGURE 1

Distribution of the Italian American Population
by Census tract, Manhattan, NY 2000

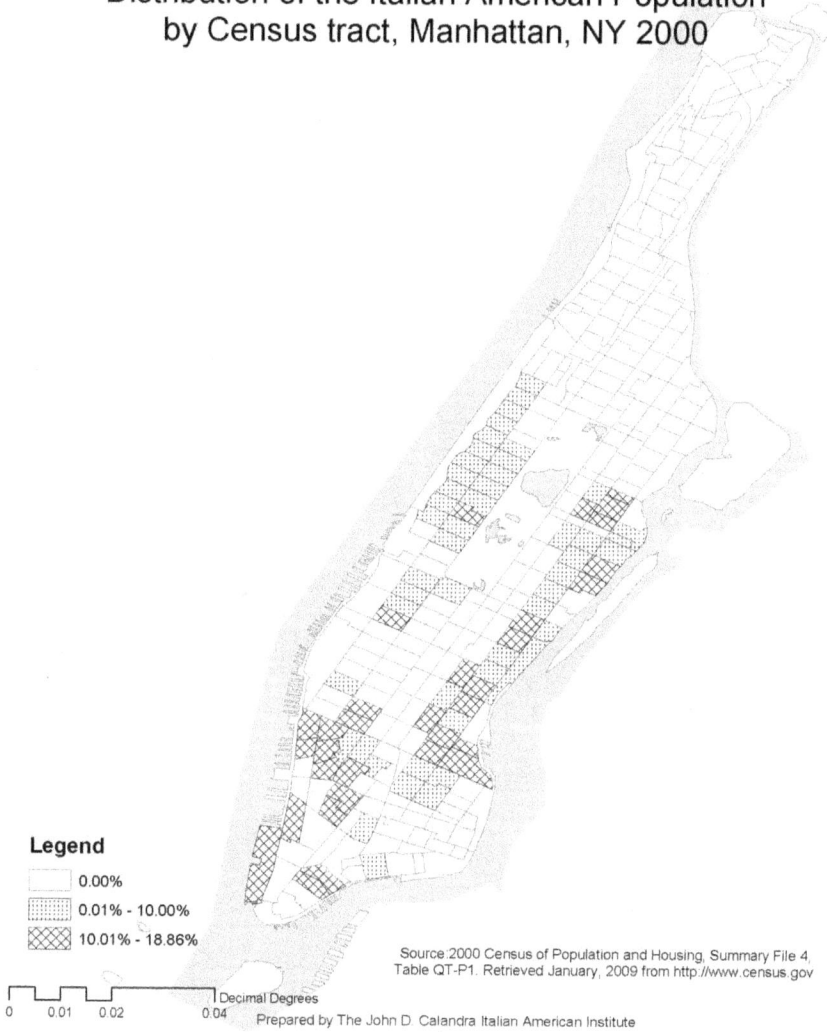

Legend

0.00%

0.01% - 10.00%

10.01% - 18.86%

Source:2000 Census of Population and Housing, Summary File 4,
Table QT-P1. Retrieved January, 2009 from http://www.census.gov

Decimal Degrees

0   0.01   0.02   0.04

Prepared by The John D. Calandra Italian American Institute

FIGURE 2

Distribution of the Italian American Population by Census tract, The Bronx, NY 2000

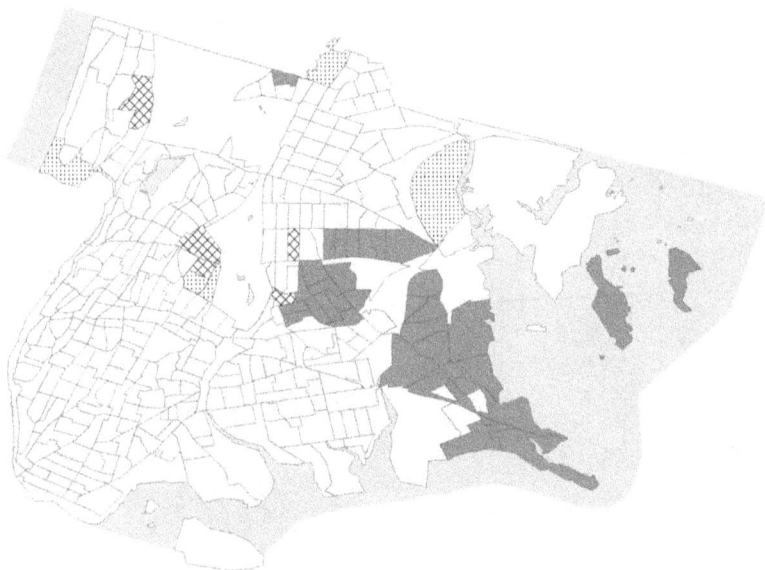

Legend

- 0.00%
- 0.01% - 10.00%
- 10.01% - 20.00%
- 20.01% - 64.72%

Decimal Degrees

0   0.01   0.02   0.04

Source:2000 Census of Population and Housing, Summary File 4, Table QT-P1. Retrieved January, 2009 from http://www.census.gov

Prepared by The John D. Calandra Italian American Institute

FIGURE 3

Distribution of the Italian American Population
by Census tract, Brooklyn, NY 2000

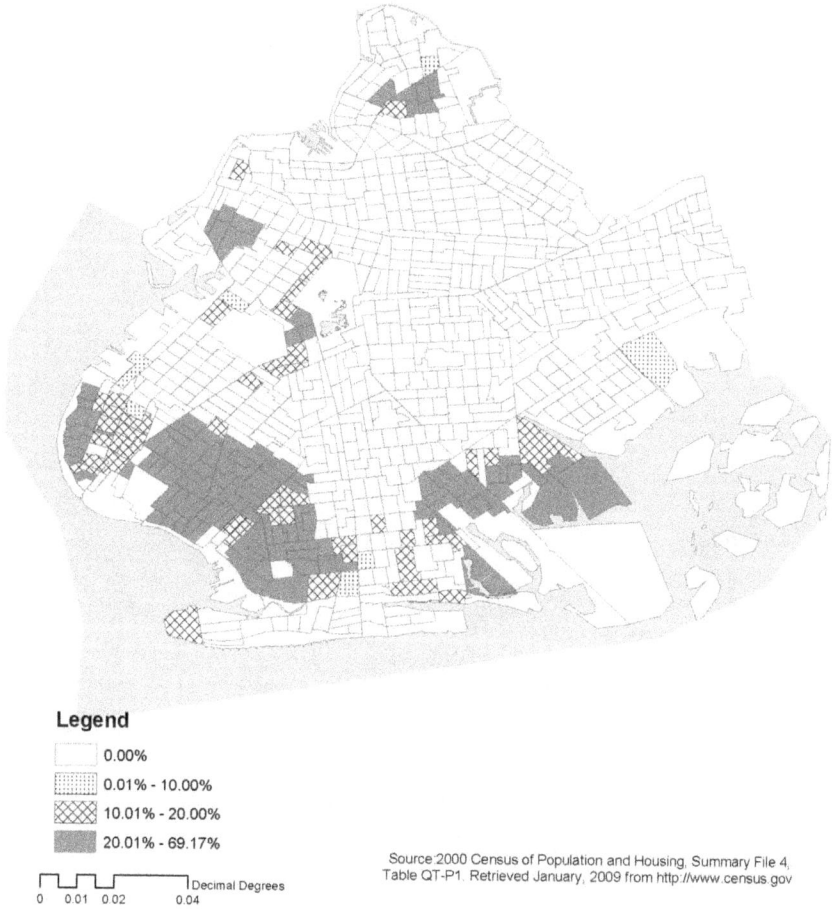

Legend

- 0.00%
- 0.01% - 10.00%
- 10.01% - 20.00%
- 20.01% - 69.17%

0   0.01   0.02   0.04   Decimal Degrees

Source:2000 Census of Population and Housing, Summary File 4, Table QT-P1. Retrieved January, 2009 from http://www.census.gov

Prepared by The John D. Calandra Italian American Institute

FIGURE 4

Distribution of the Italian American Population by Census tract, Queens, NY 2000

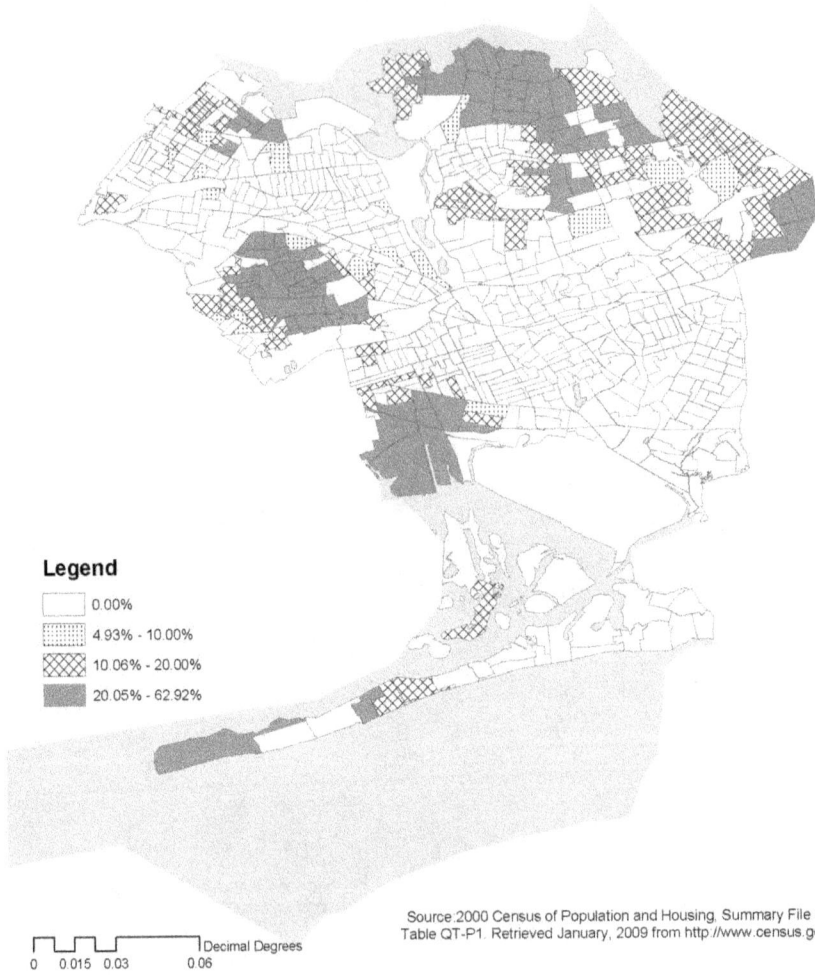

Legend

- 0.00%
- 4.93% - 10.00%
- 10.06% - 20.00%
- 20.05% - 62.92%

Source:2000 Census of Population and Housing, Summary File 4, Table QT-P1. Retrieved January, 2009 from http://www.census.gov

0   0.015   0.03   0.06   Decimal Degrees

Prepared by The John D. Calandra Italian American Institute

FIGURE 5

Distribution of the Italian American Population by Census tract, Staten Island, NY 2000

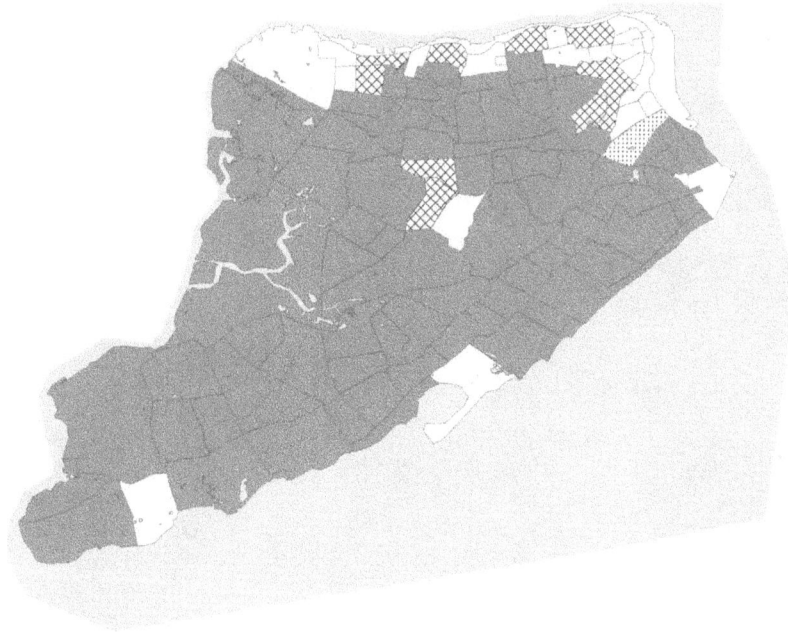

Legend

- 0.00%
- 0.01% - 10.00%
- 10.01% - 20.00%
- 20.01% - 61.30%

0   0.01 0.02   0.04 Decimal Degrees

Source:2000 Census of Population and Housing, Summary File 4, Table QT-P1. Retrieved January, 2009 from http://www.census.gov

Prepared by The John D. Calandra Italian American Institute

FIGURE 6

Distribution of the Italian American
Population by County, New York City
Tri-State Region, 2000

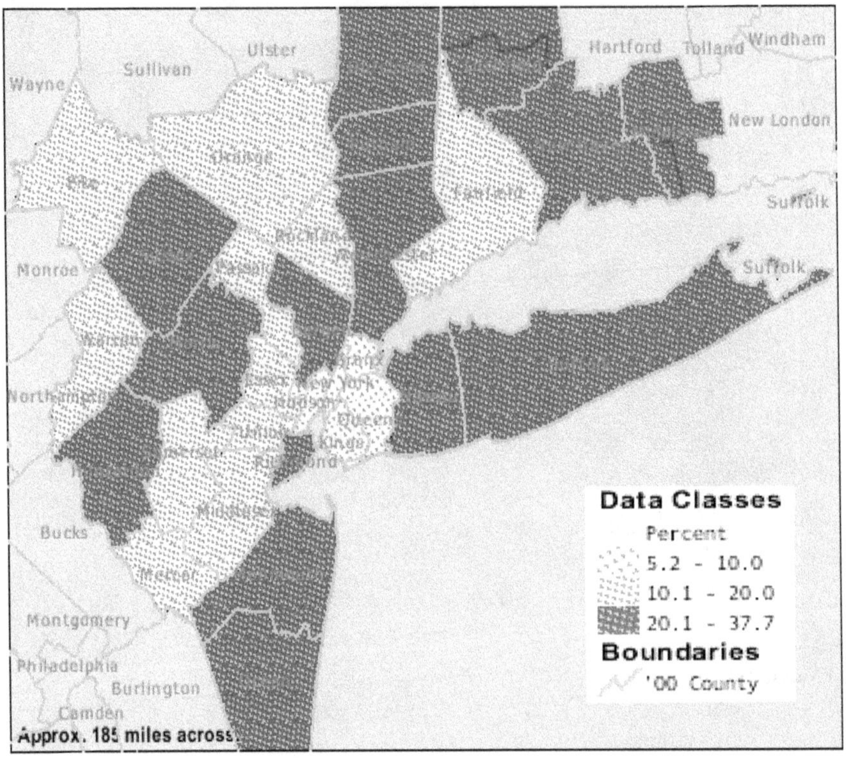

FIGURE 7

Distribution of the Italian American Population by State, United States, 2000

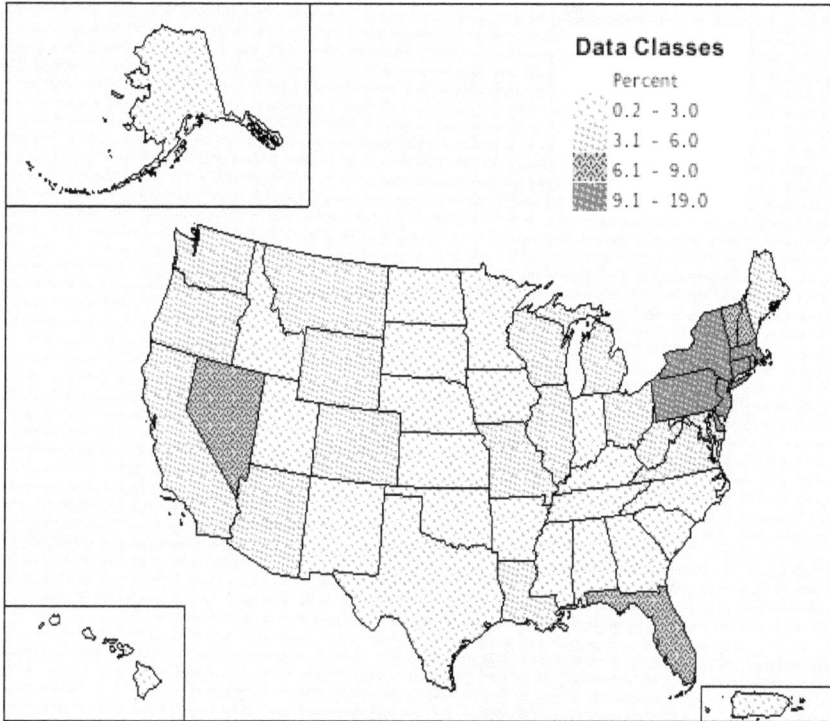

FIGURE 8

Distribution of Italian American Seniors (65 and over)
within the Italian American Population
by Census tract, Manhattan, NY 2000

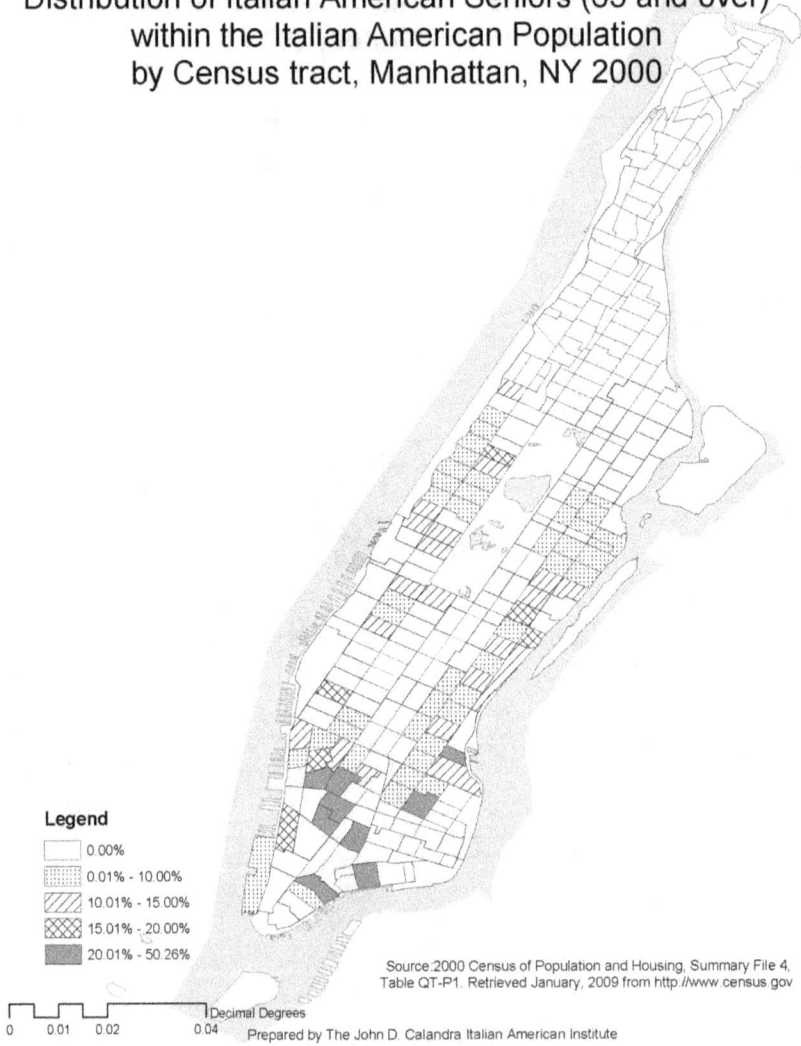

Legend

	0.00%
	0.01% - 10.00%
	10.01% - 15.00%
	15.01% - 20.00%
	20.01% - 50.26%

Source:2000 Census of Population and Housing, Summary File 4,
Table QT-P1. Retrieved January, 2009 from http://www.census.gov

Decimal Degrees

0   0.01   0.02   0.04

Prepared by The John D. Calandra Italian American Institute

FIGURE 9

Distribution of Italian American Seniors (65 and over) within the Italian American Population by Census tract, The Bronx, NY 2000

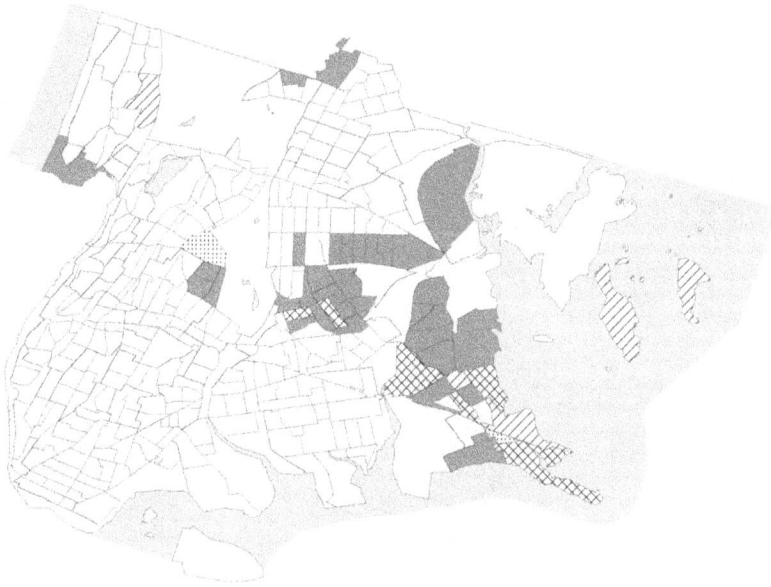

Legend

☐ 0.00%

▦ 0.01% - 10.00%

▨ 10.01% - 15.00%

▤ 15.01% - 20.00%

■ 20.01% - 53.95%

Source:2000 Census of Population and Housing, Summary File 4, Table QT-P1. Retrieved January, 2009 from http://www.census.gov

0   0.01   0.02   0.04   Decimal Degrees

Prepared by The John D. Calandra Italian American Institute

FIGURE 10

Distribution of Italian American Seniors (65 and over) within the Italian American Population by Census tract, Brooklyn, NY 2000

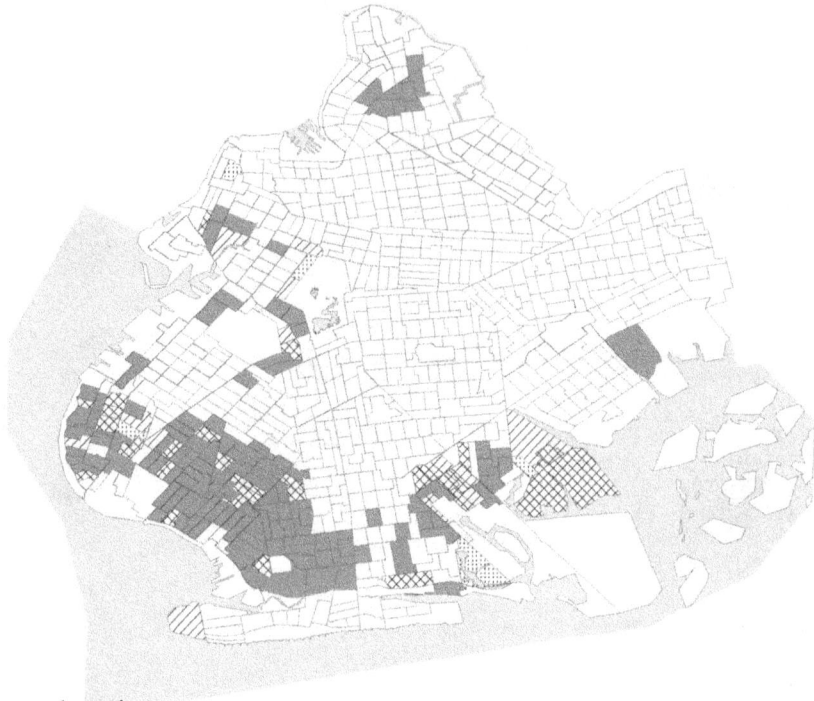

Legend

☐	0.00%
▦	0.01% - 10.00%
▨	10.01% - 15.00%
▩	15.01% - 20.00%
■	20.01% - 54.76%

0   0.01   0.02   0.04 Decimal Degrees

Source:2000 Census of Population and Housing, Summary File 4, Table QT-P1. Retrieved January, 2009 from http://www.census.gov

Prepared by The John D. Calandra Italian American Institute

FIGURE 11

Distribution of Italian American Seniors (65 and over) within the Italian American Population by Census tract, Queens, NY 2000

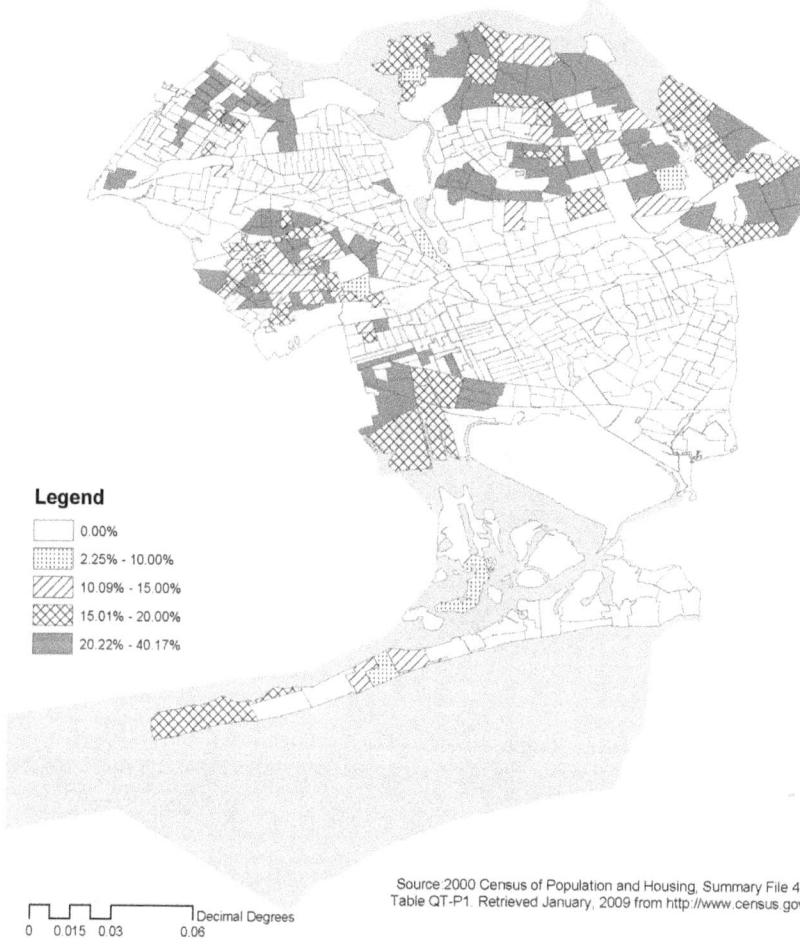

Legend

- 0.00%
- 2.25% - 10.00%
- 10.09% - 15.00%
- 15.01% - 20.00%
- 20.22% - 40.17%

Source:2000 Census of Population and Housing, Summary File 4,
Table QT-P1. Retrieved January, 2009 from http://www.census.gov

0   0.015   0.03   0.06   Decimal Degrees

Prepared by The John D. Calandra Italian American Institute

FIGURE 12

Distribution of Italian American Seniors (65 and over) within the Italian American Population by Census tract, Staten Island, NY 2000

Legend

	0.00%
	0.01% - 10.00%
	10.01% - 15.00%
	15.01% - 20.00%
	20.01% - 31.40%

0   0.01 0.02   0.04   Decimal Degrees

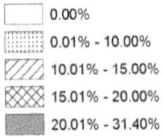

Source 2000 Census of Population and Housing, Summary File 4,
Table QT-P1. Retrieved January, 2009 from http://www.census.gov

Prepared by The John D. Calandra Italian American Institute

74

FIGURE 13

Distribution of Italian American Seniors (65 and over) within the Italian American Population by County, New York, NY 2000

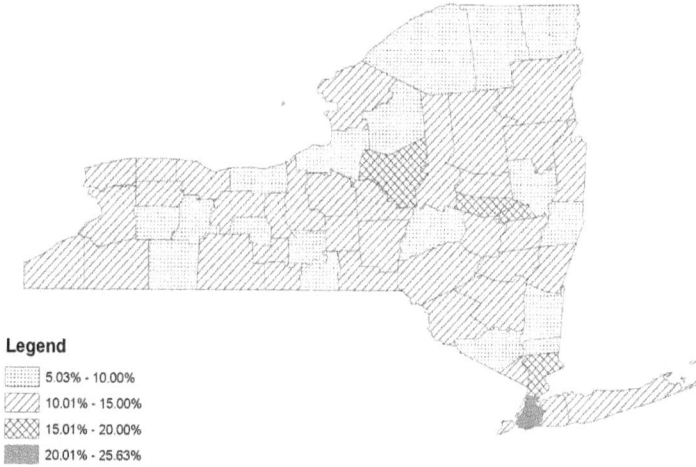

Legend

- 5.03% - 10.00%
- 10.01% - 15.00%
- 15.01% - 20.00%
- 20.01% - 25.63%

0 0.3 0.6 1.2 Decimal Degrees

Source:2000 Census of Population and Housing, Summary File 4, Table QT-P1. Retrieved January, 2009 from http://www.census.gov

Prepared by The John D. Calandra Italian American Institute

FIGURE 14

Distribution of Italian American Seniors (65 and over)
within the Italian American Population
by County, New Jersey, NJ 2000

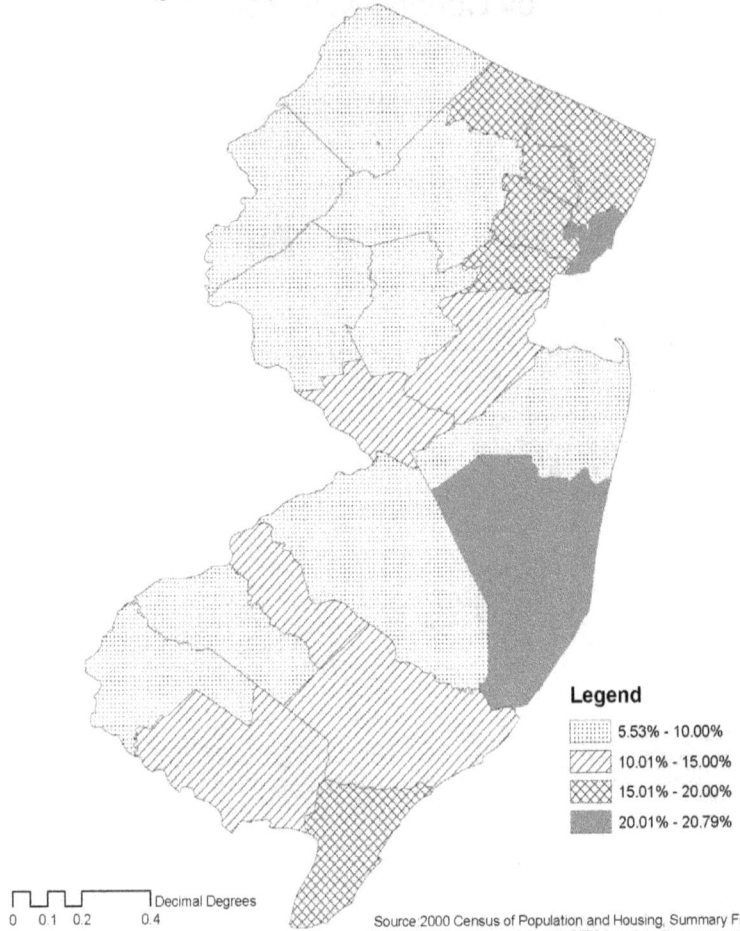

Legend

░	5.53% - 10.00%
▨	10.01% - 15.00%
▧	15.01% - 20.00%
■	20.01% - 20.79%

Decimal Degrees
0   0.1   0.2   0.4

Source:2000 Census of Population and Housing, Summary File 4, Table QT-P1. Retrieved January, 2009 from http://www.census.gov

Prepared by The John D. Calandra Italian American Institute

FIGURE 15

Distribution of Italian American Seniors (65 and over) within the Italian American Population by County, Connecticut, CT 2000

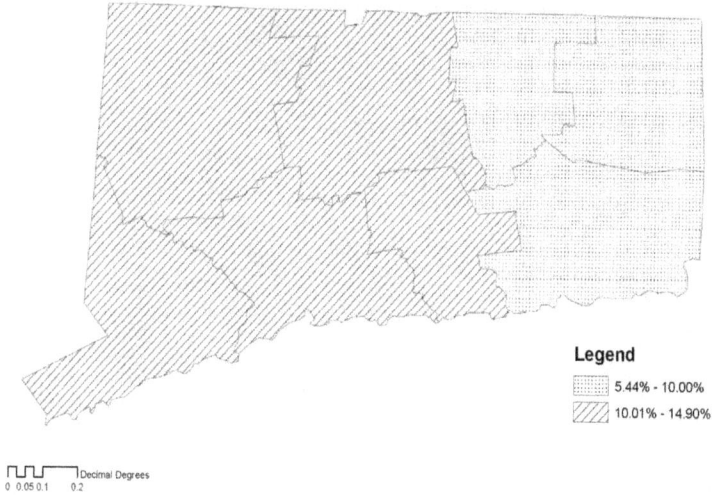

Legend
5.44% - 10.00%
10.01% - 14.90%

Decimal Degrees
0 0.05 0.1   0.2

Source:2000 Census of Population and Housing, Summary File 4,
Table QT-P1. Retrieved January, 2009 from http://www.census.gov

Prepared by The John D. Calandra Italian American Institute

FIGURE 16

Distribution of Italian American Seniors (65 and over) within the Italian American Population by State, USA, NY 2000

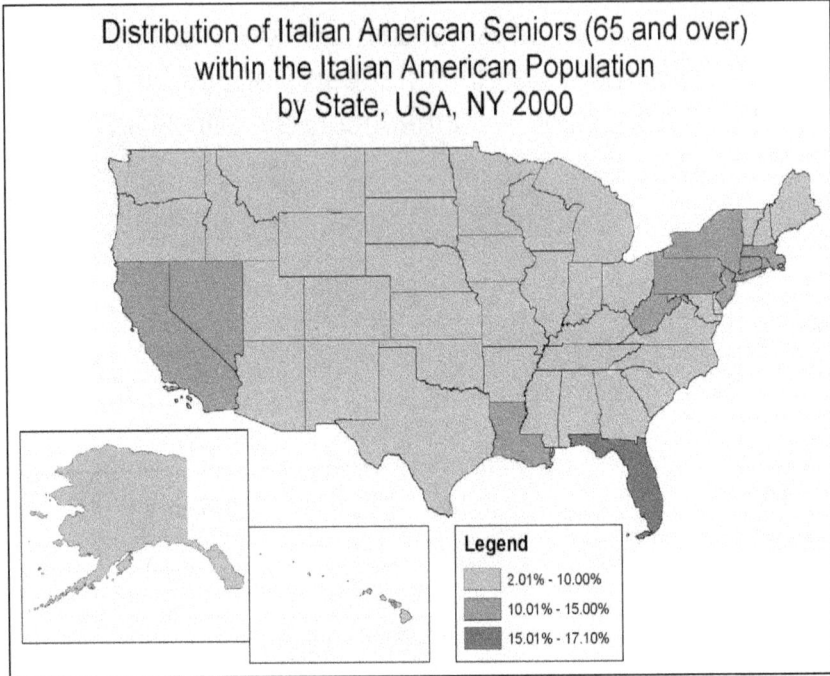

Legend

2.01% - 10.00%

10.01% - 15.00%

15.01% - 17.10%

Source 2000 Census of Population and Housing, Summary File 4,
Retrieval January 2009 from http://www.census.gov

Prepared by the John D. Calandra Italian American Institute

APPENDIX B
TABLES

TABLE 1

UNITED STATES – 2000	Ages 5-17	Ages 18+	Total
Total U.S Population (age 5+)	53,096,003	209,279,149	262,375,152
Italian speakers in U.S. (age 5+)	68,029	940,341	1,008,370
Population of Italian Ancestry in U.S. (age 5+)	3,184,637	11,353,835	14,538,472
% of total pop (age 5+) of Italian ancestry	6.00%	5.43%	5.54%
% of Italian pop (age 5+) who spoke Italian	2.14%	8.28%	6.94%

Source: Census 2000 SF 3 and SF 4

TABLE 2

UNITED STATES – 2000-2006	2000	2006	Difference 2000 to 2006	% change
Total U.S Population (5+ years)	262,375,152	279,012,712	16,637,560	6.34%

Italian – U.S.	2000	2006	Difference 2000 to 2006	% change
Italian speakers in U.S. (age 5+ years)	1,008,370	828,524	-179,846	-17.84%
Italian population in U.S. (age 5+ years)	14,538,472	16,509,824	1,971,352	13.56%
% of Italian Americans speaking Italian at home	6.94%	5.02%		

Source: Census 2000 SF 3 and SF 4; 2006 American Community Survey

TABLE 3

TRI-STATE AREA – 2000	Ages 5-17	Ages 18+	Total
Total Tri-State Population (age 5+)	3,802,455	15,972,983	19,775,438
Italian speakers in Tri-State (age 5+)	25,952	352,671	378,623
Population of Italian Ancestry in Tri-State (age 5+)	621,272	2,534,122	3,155,394
% of total pop (age 5+) of Italian ancestry	16.34%	15.87%	15.96%
% of Italian pop (age 5+) who spoke Italian	4.18%	13.92%	12.00%

Source: Census 2000 SF 3 and SF 4

TABLE 4

TRI-STATE – 2000-2006	2000	2006	Difference from 2000 to 2006	% change
Total Tri-State Population (5+ years)	19,775,438	17,556,103	-2,219,335	-11.22%

Italian – Tri-state	2000	2006	Difference from 2000 to 2006	% change
Italian speakers in Tri-State (age 5+ years)	378,623	269,525	-109,098	-28.81%
Italian population in Tri-State (age 5+ years)	3,155,394	2,678,576	-476,818	-15.11%
% of Italian Americans speaking Italian at home	12.00%	10.06%		

Source: Census 2000 SF 3 and SF 4; 2006 American Community Survey

TABLE 5

NEW YORK CITY – 2000	ages 5-17	ages 18+	Total
Total NYC Population (age 5+)	1,397,597	6,078,005	7,475,602
Italian speakers in NYC (age 5+)	9,072	130,626	139,698
Population of Italian Ancestry in NYC (age 5+)	88,642	569,937	658,579
% of total pop. (age 5+) of Italian ancestry	6.34%	9.38%	8.81%
% of Italian pop. (age 5+) who spoke Italian	10.23%	22.92%	21.21%

Source: Census 2000 SF 3 and SF 4

TABLE 6

NEW YORK CITY – 2000-2006	2000	2006	Difference 2000 to 2006	% change
Total NYC Population (5+ years)	7,475,602	7,637,820	162,218	2.17%
Italian speakers NYC (age 5+ years)	139,698	109,817	-29,881	-21.39%
Italian population in NYC (age 5+ years)	658,579	635,290	-23,289	-3.54%
% of Italian Americans speaking Italian at home	21.21%	17.29%		

Source: Census 2000 SF 3 and SF 4; 2006 American Community Survey

TABLE 7

Those who speak Italian at home: Percent of respondents who can speak a non-English language, and who also use that language as their primary home language			
Respondent speaks non-English language at home?	Italian speakers	Non-Italian "foreign" language speakers	Speakers of a language other than English in U.S.
Speaks the language at home	33.3%	41.7%	41.3%
Does not speak the language at home	66.7%	58.3%	58.7%
Total	100.0%	100.0%	100.0%

Source: General Social Survey 2000-2006

TABLE 8

Where language was acquired	Italian speakers	Non-Italian "foreign" language speakers	Speakers of another language other than English
Childhood Home	66.0%	52.5%	53.1%
School	20.0%	32.9%	32.3%
Elsewhere	14.0%	14.6%	14.6%
Total	100.0%	100.0%	100.0%

Where did Italian speakers learn to speak Italian?
Percent of "foreign" language speakers in the U.S. that learned the language at home, at school, or elsewhere.

Source: General Social Survey 2000-2006

TABLE 9

Who speaks Italian?
Countries of family origin represented among Italian speaking respondents

Country of Family Origin	Percent of Italian speakers in the U.S.
Italy	72.3%
Germany	8.5%
Puerto Rico	6.4%
Ireland	4.3%
France	2.1%
Mexico	2.1%
Spain	2.1%
Switzerland	2.1%
Total	99.9%

Source: General Social Survey 2000-2006

TABLE 10

How many Italian Americans speak a language other than English?

Speak a Language Other than English	No Italian ancestry	Italian ancestry	Overall
Yes	25.7%	26.7%	25.7%
No	74.3%	73.3%	74.3%
Total	100.0%	100.0%	100.0%

Source: General Social Survey 2000-2006

TABLE 11

Italians in New York, Northern New Jersey, and Connecticut by County, 2000			
County	Total population	Total Italians	% Italian
Richmond County, New York	443,728	167,086	37.7%
Putnam County, New York	95,745	30,441	31.8%
Suffolk County, New York	1,419,369	408,572	28.8%
Ocean County, New Jersey	510,916	129,044	25.3%
New Haven County, Connecticut	824,008	201,069	24.4%
Nassau County, New York	1,334,544	319,602	23.9%
Monmouth County, New Jersey	615,301	142,727	23.2%
Morris County, New Jersey	470,212	107,123	22.8%
Sussex County, New Jersey	144,166	31,962	22.2%
Bergen County, New Jersey	884,118	194,614	22.0%
Litchfield County, Connecticut	182,193	39,477	21.7%
Dutchess County, New York	280,150	60,645	21.6%
Middlesex County, Connecticut	155,071	32,858	21.2%
Westchester County, New York	923,459	192,226	20.8%
Hunterdon County, New Jersey	121,989	25,086	20.6%
Pike County, Pennsylvania	46,302	9,138	19.7%
Orange County, New York	341,367	64,450	18.9%
Somerset County, New Jersey	297,490	55,612	18.7%
Warren County, New Jersey	102,437	19,129	18.7%
Fairfield County, Connecticut	882,567	159,785	18.1%
Rockland County, New York	286,753	48,802	17.0%

TABLE 11

(cont.)

Italians in New York, Northern New Jersey, and Connecticut by County, 2000			
County	Total population	Total Italians	% Italian
Passaic County, New Jersey	489,049	81,205	16.6%
Middlesex County, New Jersey	750,162	120,402	16.1%
Mercer County, New Jersey	350,761	54,092	15.4%
Union County, New Jersey	522,541	70,914	13.6%
Essex County, New Jersey	793,633	92,389	11.6%
Hudson County, New Jersey	608,975	60,746	10.0%
Queens County, New York	2,229,379	187,540	8.4%
Kings County, New York	2,465,326	183,868	7.5%
New York County, New York	1,537,195	84,956	5.5%
Bronx County, New York	1,332,650	69,289	5.2%

TABLE 12

Italians in the United States, by State, 2000				
State	Total population	Total Italians	% Italian	Rank
Rhode Island	1048319	199077	19.0%	1
Connecticut	3405565	634364	18.6%	2
New Jersey	8414350	1503637	17.9%	3
New York	18976457	2737115	14.4%	4
Massachusetts	6349097	860079	13.5%	5
Pennsylvania	12281054	1418465	11.6%	6
Delaware	783600	72677	9.3%	7
New Hampshire	1235786	105610	8.5%	8
Nevada	1998257	132515	6.6%	9
Vermont	608827	38835	6.4%	10
Florida	15982378	1003967	6.3%	11
Illinois	12419293	744274	6.0%	12
Ohio	11353140	675749	6.0%	13
Maryland	5296486	267573	5.1%	14
Colorado	4301261	201782	4.7%	15
Maine	1274923	58866	4.6%	16
Michigan	9938444	450950	4.5%	17
Arizona	5130632	224787	4.4%	18
Louisiana	4468976	195561	4.4%	19
California	33871648	1450854	4.3%	20
West Virginia	1808344	69935	3.9%	21
Virginia	7078515	257129	3.6%	22
Oregon	3421399	111462	3.3%	23
Washington	5894121	191440	3.2%	24
Wisconsin	5363675	172561	3.2%	25
Missouri	5595211	176202	3.1%	26
Montana	902195	28031	3.1%	27
Wyoming	493782	15286	3.1%	28
Alaska	626932	17944	2.9%	29
Idaho	1293953	34553	2.7%	30
Utah	2233169	57512	2.6%	31

TABLE 12
(cont.)

Italians in the United States, by State, 2000				
State	Total population	Total Italians	% Italian	Rank
Nebraska	1711263	42979	2.5%	32
New Mexico	1819046	43218	2.4%	33
Indiana	6080485	141486	2.3%	34
Minnesota	4919479	111254	2.3%	35
North Carolina	8049313	181982	2.3%	36
District of Columbia	572059	12587	2.2%	37
South Carolina	4012012	81377	2.0%	38
Georgia	8186453	163218	2.0%	39
Kansas	2688418	50729	1.9%	40
Hawaii	1211537	22094	1.8%	41
Texas	20851820	363339	1.7%	42
Iowa	2926324	49441	1.7%	43
Tennessee	5689283	94402	1.7%	44
Kentucky	4041769	62374	1.5%	45
Oklahoma	3450654	49970	1.4%	46
Mississippi	2844658	40401	1.4%	47
Arkansas	2673400	34674	1.3%	48
Alabama	4447100	56220	1.3%	49
South Dakota	754844	7541	1.0%	50
North Dakota	642200	5328	0.8%	51

INDEX

ABOUT THE AUTHORS

CHRISTINE GAMBINO, Assistant for Demographic Studies at the John D. Calandra Institute, holds a B.A. in Psychology from University of California at San Diego, an M.A. in Applied Developmental Psychology from Fordham University, and is currently a doctoral student at Fordham. A former researcher, statistician, and instructor at Fordham University and New York University, Ms. Gambino has engaged in research at the Administration for Children's Services (ACS), Agenda for Children Tomorrow (ACT), Lighthouse International, UCSD Community Pediatrics, and the U.S. Department of Energy. Her research interests include Italian-American student achievement levels, and evaluating the effects of poverty on at-risk youth.

VINCENZO MILIONE, Ph.D., is Director of Demographic Studies for The John D. Calandra Italian American Institute of Queens College, The City University of New York. He is also responsible for social science research on Italian Americans, as well as conducting institutional research for faculty, administrative staff, and students. He has conducted research on educational and occupational achievements, Italian language studies, high school non-completion rates, negative media portrayals, Italy/U.S. student exchange programs and global Italian *diaspora* migration. Federal Judge Constance Baker Motley designated Dr. Milione a technical civil rights expert for affirmative action. He has also helped to establish the Anthony and Eleanor De Francis multimillion-scholarship fund for Italian American students.

NOTES

NOTES

www.ingramcontent.com/pod-product-compliance
Lightning Source LLC
Chambersburg PA
CBHW081659270326
41933CB00017B/3227